THE FABULOUS FUTURE

AMERICA in 1980

The Fabulous Future

AMERICA in 1980

as seen by

DAVID SARNOFF	*Chairman, RCA*
JOHN VON NEUMANN	*Member, AEC*
GEORGE MEANY	*President, AFL-CIO*
NATHAN M. PUSEY	*President, Harvard University*
EARL WARREN	*Chief Justice of the U.S.*
CRAWFORD H. GREENEWALT	*President, du Pont Co.*
GEORGE M. HUMPHREY	*Secretary of the Treasury*
ADLAI E. STEVENSON	*Presidential Candidate*
ROBERT E. SHERWOOD	*Playwright and Historian*
CHARLES P. TAFT	*Federal Council of Churches*
HENRY R. LUCE	*Editor-in-Chief, Time Inc.*

With an Introduction by the Editors of FORTUNE

Essay Index Reprint Series

BOOKS FOR LIBRARIES PRESS
FREEPORT, NEW YORK

INTERNATIONAL STANDARD BOOK NUMBER:
0-8369-2315-4

LIBRARY OF CONGRESS CATALOG CARD NUMBER:
79-134077
3-6-74

PRINTED IN THE UNITED STATES OF AMERICA

The Fabulous Future

INTRODUCTION

Since man is a rational being he has always employed his reasoning powers to project his thoughts into the future. In the past these efforts have generally taken two forms. On the one hand, seers and soothsayers have, since ancient times, sought to predict the course of human events, while religious prophets have attempted to discern the shape of eternity. Philosophers and ideologists, on the other hand, have been less concerned with predictions of what will happen than with designing blueprints of what *ought* to happen. The Forecasters have tended on the whole to sell Man short, while the Planners frequently have attributed to Man a perfection of character that he has yet to demonstrate.

In 1980, according to H. G. Wells' *The Shape of Things to Come*, the Pope will just have been gassed, the One World-State declared, and a government "to rule not only the planet but the human will" will be taking shape. According to Spengler the hundred years after World War I was to be a century of "Contending States"—a dismal prophecy that has yet to be disproved even though at the moment there is peace on earth for the first time in fifty years.

In regard to scientific progress, most men in each generation have failed to visualize the speed of technical advance in succeeding generations. In 1844, for example, the U.S. Commissioner of Patents declared, "The advancement of the arts from year to year taxes our credulity and seems to presage the arrival of that period when further improvements must end." Fifty years ago, there were learned scientists arguing that man would never be able to fly, and brain surgeons

5

predicting that the "mind would crumble under the speed of automobiles." Who took Jules Verne's fantasy of *20,000 Leagues Under the Sea* seriously when it was first published? Until recently only the devotees of science fiction and comics laid much store in rocket ships, guided missiles, and such. How long was it to have taken Man to progress from fission to fusion of the atom? There is a geometry in scientific progress that excites—and apparently often stuns—the imagination.

These are the perils in prophecy. But for those concerned with the future well being of America it is heartening to note that virtually all the recent economic forecasts have been highly optimistic. And, perhaps because most of the forecasts project recent trends into the future, they tend to be remarkably uniform. To take just one recent example, FORTUNE projects for the average American family unit a 1980 spendable income in excess of $8,000. (The figure is now $4,400.) Moreover this average income will be earned in a work week of only thirty-five hours (as compared to today's forty-one).

Such projections are more than pie in the sky. They are based on a demonstrable hypothesis that the U.S. output per man-hour, which has been increasing at an average of two per cent a year for nearly a century, will probably increase by an average of *three* per cent a year over the next twenty-five years. The implications of this 50 per cent rise in the rate of productivity increase are staggering. For one thing it means that production per man-hour in the U.S. will double in less than twenty-four years.

Given this future prospect of great wealth and power, thoughtful men will ask what other goals the U.S. should strive toward during the coming quarter-century. What kind of world should America be trying to bring about by 1980? What problems will be met and with what posture will they be faced? THE FABULOUS FUTURE, less concerned with what

America *will* be like in 1980 than with what it *should* be like, takes this subject for its own.

The special competence its distinguished contributors bring to such an examination needs no underlining. Their leadership in our national life makes it inevitable that American hopes and aims should be their special concern. This indeed was the particular reason they were invited to contribute to this FORTUNE series.

The chapters that follow were first presented in FORTUNE during 1955 to mark the anniversary of Fortune's twenty-fifth year of publication. From the first it was clear that the results of this collaboration were of much more than contemporary interest, and the desirability of their collection in more permanent form than a periodical can offer became increasingly evident.

Four months after the publication of his article, Robert Sherwood, eminent historian and playwright, died of a heart attack in New York. His article, one of the last published during his lifetime, begins on page 147 of this volume.

The Editors gratefully acknowledge their debt to their successful authors, and trust that the close attention accorded them by FORTUNE's readers, as well as the publication of this book, will help to repay it. The reader who for the first time meets these distinguished Americans between the covers of THE FABULOUS FUTURE will find that they have much to say that is important—and that they say it well.

The Editors of FORTUNE

Contents

THE FABULOUS FUTURE

AMERICA in 1980

DAVID SARNOFF
Chairman, Radio Corporation of America

In 1930, David Sarnoff, self-educated and then thirty-eight, was elected president of the Radio Corporation of America. That year RCA acquired the radio manufacturing rights and facilities of General Electric and Westinghouse. Since then RCA has prospered mightily (its sales have risen from $137 million to more than $900 million) and the name of Sarnoff has become, if not synonymous, at least indelibly linked with electronic progress. As early as 1923 he informed the directors of RCA, "I believe that television, which is the technical name for seeing as well as hearing by radio, will come to pass in due course. . . ." As active in citizenship as in electronics, Brigadier General Sarnoff (he won the rank for service at SHAEF in World War II) recently headed the Citizens' Advisory Commission on Manpower Utilization in the Armed Forces. General Sarnoff has a consuming interest in the future; at the dedication of the David Sarnoff Research Center at Princeton, he declared, "The challenge of tomorrow fascinates me much more than the achievements of yesterday."

12

The Fabulous Future

BY DAVID SARNOFF

What is likely to be the special character of the quarter-century ahead of us? Personally, I am convinced that it will be a period of drastic decision. It will be filled with events that, taken together, may well determine the direction and even the duration of man's destiny on this planet.

That an avalanche of advances will be forthcoming in the sphere of science and technology is not a matter of surmise. The new types of energy released by the atom and controlled by the electron have already proved highly effective. The features of vital technical growths can be discerned in number-less embryos in the womb of science: our amazing network of research laboratories.

But these features will be matched by even more significant developments in the political, social, and moral spheres. Indeed, the pressures of technical changes will themselves intensify problems of adjustment, forcing us to seek solutions in line with our ideals of a good society.

Long-stagnant races and continents have awakened to an awareness of their rights, needs, and latent strengths. Long-accepted ways of life and codes of conduct are being menaced by a new barbarism that already dominates a third of the human race. A hunger for faith and salvation, for age-old values beyond the material and the temporal, gnaws at the mind and spirit of man.

This means that the coming quarter-century will be crowded with crises and climaxes. Forces that have been gathering impetus since the turn of the century will find

13

vigorous and perhaps explosive expression. The tensions built up in our own generation are too great to be indefinitely contained. We will be confronted with great challenges that will call for dramatic commitments on our part.

If the destinies were already written in the stars and beyond mortal control, there would be little point in talking about them. But I am convinced, as are most people, that our destinies are, in large part, subject to our own volition. It is understandable that at times we have been frightened and bewildered. But we do have a choice: we can grovel in terror before the mighty forces of science and historic adjustment, even as savage man groveled before lightning and other natural phenomena. Or we can face those forces with courage, determination, and calm intelligence. We do have such a choice because we are not the passive objects but the active manipulators of those forces.

1   The Technological Age

For those of us who view history as a fascinating spectacle, the prospect of the coming quarter-century is exhilarating. It is as if we were privileged not only to see but to participate in centuries of development telescoped into a brief span. Of one thing we can be sure: the segment of time between now and 1980 will not be dull. It will make heavy demands upon courage and character, upon wisdom and good will. And I have confidence that we can meet those demands, provided we approach our tasks not in fear but with faith in ourselves and in the strength of our freedoms.

The dominant physical fact in the next quarter-century will be technological progress unprecedented in kind and in volume. In relation to the total history of the human race, the last hundred years have been no more than a split second. Yet they have compassed more technological achievement than the millennia that preceded. The harnessing of electricity to the purposes of light, power, and communication; the demonstration of the germ theory of disease; discovery and application of the electron; invention of radio and television; development of anesthetics; the exploration of genes and mutations; invention of motor vehicles; evolution of the assembly line and other mass-production techniques; proliferation of organic chemistry; the splitting of the atom; development of antibiotics; the vast expansion of the known and measured universe of stars and galaxies—these are only the highlights of recent progress. On the day when the first issue of FORTUNE was published, television, nuclear energy, jet planes, penicillin, nylon and dacron fabrics were unknown or incubating in laboratories.

The quantity of the new powers and products and processes at man's disposal is important; but even more important is *the increasing speed* at which these things have come. It is not a case of continued increase but of continued acceleration of increase. We need only project the curve into the future to realize that we are merely on the threshold of the technological age.

A recent statement by the General Electric Co., referring especially to electronic and atomic energy, declared: "All these fields . . . are so promising that we expect to produce more in the next ten years than in all the previous seventy-five years of our existence." The figures may vary, but the same pattern of rapid growth holds true for the Radio Corporation of America and for American enterprise as a whole.

THREE ANNIVERSARY PRESENTS

There is no longer margin for doubt that whatever the mind of man visualizes, the genius of modern science can turn into functioning fact. I have seen this demonstrated again and again. A current example will show what I mean.

In 1951, on the occasion of the forty-fifth anniversary of my association with radio, I suggested to the scientists of the RCA research laboratory in Princeton, New Jersey, which bears my name, that they invent three "presents" for me by the time the fiftieth anniversary came around in 1956. I asked, first, for a magnetic tape recorder of television programs; second, an all-electronic air conditioner; and third, a true amplifier of light.

The scientists smiled. "He certainly can ask for the impossible," one of them later remarked. But the thrilling part of the story is that before half the five-year period had passed, the scientists had actually produced one of the "presents," the magnetic tape recorder of black-and-white and color television programs; and they had made such substantial progress on the other two that their early realization now appears most promising.

We are now engaged in the development of a new form of light—*electronic light,* which is the keystone of the light amplifier under development in RCA laboratories. Already I have seen this light amplification, experimentally, in ratios of more than twenty times the original; and further progress is certain to be made. When that number twenty reaches 100, we shall have a practical amplifier of light—produced directly within a thin layer of electronically active material.

The potentials for practical use of this development will surely be greater than we can now foresee. This can safely be said of almost any new invention. When Faraday first produced an electric current, neither he nor his contemporaries could visualize the amazing future he had unlocked. Neither did Marconi dream of broadcasting and television when he succeeded in sending the first faint wireless telegraph signal through the air.

Electronic light will eventually provide startling substitutes for present types of illumination and thus will change the very appearance of our homes, stores, factories, streets, and cities. Electric light will have been freed from the prison of a vacuum bulb. It will obsolete the television tube of today, while bringing bigger and sharper pictures in color as well as in black and white. Light amplification is expected to lead to devices that will make not only photography but vision possible in the darkness, and to enlarge immensely our visual penetration of outer astronomic space. It may well reduce and in time cancel out one of the perils of night driving by taking the glare out of light.

I have enlarged on the implications of a single research project in a single laboratory in order to suggest the fabulous dimensions of the teeming novelties now gestating in hundreds of laboratories, large and small.

''ATOMS FOR PEACE''

The released energies of the atom, though born in war and baptized in destruction, are already being funneled to man's constructive purposes. Because nuclear power is so recent and impressive, we have not yet digested it psychologically as we have earlier miracles. The real mission of science should be to create, not destroy. While the first atomic propulsion has been assigned to a submarine, it can be taken for granted that before 1980 ships, aircraft, locomotives, and even automobiles will be atomically fueled.

The era of nuclear power for peaceable civilian purposes

is already at hand. It dawned in America when President Eisenhower waved a neutron wand in Denver, Colorado, that broke ground at Shippingport, Pennsylvania, for the first commercial plant powered by atomic energy. The first nuclear-power plant will surely rank with the first steam engine, the first electric motor, Morse's first telegraph message, Edison's first electric lamp, and Marconi's first wireless message as milestones of man's material progress.

Two years ago the Radio Corporation of America publicly demonstrated an atomic battery that gives promise of many useful services. Only a minute amount of electric current was generated: barely enough to send the short telegraphic message I had the privilege of tapping out—"Atoms for peace." But the potentials of that event are enormous. This was no longer the use of atomic energy to make steam to make electric current—it was the direct conversion of nuclear energy into electricity.

I do not hesitate to forecast that atomic batteries will be commonplace long before 1980. The waste products from the fast-multiplying commercial reactors will make available abundant captive radiation for direct conversion into electricity. Small atomic generators, installed in homes and industrial plants, will provide power for years and ultimately for a lifetime without recharging. Coal, oil, and gas will be increasingly displaced as fuel by nuclear energy, but will in turn be devoted to other uses by new developments of chemistry and engineering.

THINGS TO COME

Other sources of energy—the sun, the tides, and the winds—are certain to be developed beyond present expectations. New materials by the score—metals, fabrics, woods, glass—will be added to the hundreds of synthetics and plastics already available through our capacity to rearrange the structure of matter.

Fresh water, purified from the briny seas, will enable us to make deserts flourish and to open to human habitation immense surfaces of the globe now sterile or inaccessible. Tidelands and the ocean floors beyond, already being tapped for oil, will be increasingly mined for other materials and harvested for chemical and food resources.

Even guided missiles, transcontinental and transoceanic, will find vital civilian uses. They will transport mail and other types of freight over great distances, guided into terminal hangars within minutes after their take-off. Pilotless aircraft for passengers, too, are within the realm of the possible. Great fleets of personal helicopters and other planes will make the principal airways almost as busy as the highways on the ground; and electronic controls will ensure safe travel in both dimensions.

Medicine can look to incalculable aid from science and technology. Already diagnosis, prognosis, therapy, and surgery have begun to make important use of nuclear radiation and electronic devices: the electron microscope, for instance. Such uses will expand enormously by 1980. Similarly, techniques for learning faster and better will be opened up by color television, improved means of communication, electronic magnification, and other novel processes.

The era of "automation" is upon us. Electronic machines will not only compute, remember, and file information—tasks they have already taken on for business offices, banks, factories, and research laboratories—but they will perform more and more routine jobs now handled by people. Production especially will lean ever more heavily on electronics in the immediate years ahead. Automatic equipment will take much of the drudgery and spoilage out of manufacture. It will do the jobs of selecting, testing, checking, and handling raw materials and finished products. The goods thus produced will then be stored and inventoried electronically.

Some of the innovations will call for a change in products or methods of operation in some of today's business organizations. However, the whole history of our American economy proves that such changes spell progress; eventually many new jobs will be created for every job canceled out. The contrast between the millions employed by the automotive and related industries and the employment provided by the blacksmith shops they displaced is an overworked example, but it tells the basic story.

The temptation, at least for someone who, like myself, has been in touch all his life with such spiraling wonders, is to continue the inventory of what is coming. The very fact that electronics and atomics are unfolding simultaneously is a portent of the amazing changes ahead. Never before have two such mighty forces been unleashed at the same time. Together they are certain to dwarf the industrial revolutions brought about by steam and electricity. There is no element of material progress we know today—in the biological and chemical fields, in atomics and electronics, in engineering and physics —that will not seem, from the vantage point of 1980, a fumbling prelude.

NEW GRACE TO LIFE

We have a right to make the same kind of projection for social progress, though with far less assurance. Let us, therefore, provide such assurance by setting our sights high. The material triumphs now at our disposal and the greater ones to come must be translated into a happier life for mankind everywhere. We must give a clear right-of-way to the things that are good, beautiful, and enriching.

High among our goals must be greater mutual tolerance among races and nationalities. We cannot wholly weed out the primeval prejudices and fears in the jungle undergrowth of the human mind. But we can remove some and neutralize the effects of the rest.

The reduction of crime—by individuals and by nations—also deserves priority in our hopes and plans. The ever more plentiful supplies of food and goods, higher standards of living and education and health—these should make the containment of violence easier during the coming twenty-five years.

Automation and other aspects of scientific advance will, as a matter of course, put a premium on brains rather than brawn. Even now, in America, illiteracy has become more of a handicap in life than most physical handicaps. The demands for mental competence will be vastly enlarged. One hopes that by 1980 a decent education (though I recognize that no two of us will agree on definitions here) will have become as indispensable as a decent suit of clothes.

Leisure, of course, will be greatly extended. A much shorter work week will no doubt prevail in 1980, and another ten or fifteen years will have been added to the average life span. Cancer, polio, tuberculosis, and an array of other scourges will have been consigned to the same limbo as cholera, typhus, and other great killers of the past.

Not labor but leisure will be the great problem in the decades ahead. That prospect should be accepted as a God-given opportunity to add dimensions of enjoyment and grace to life. We have reason to foresee a fantastic rise in demand for and appreciation of the better, and perhaps the best, in art, music, and letters.

In small things and large, in greater conveniences and a greater recognition of our common humanity, the quarter-century awaits us in a mood of welcome. We must resolve to fulfill its thrilling promises. Should we fail, the fault will not be with science and technology but with ourselves.

2   Progress, a Chain Reaction

The most futile intellectual exercise is the discussion as to whether an industrialized society is "desirable." We might as reasonably argue whether the tides and the seasons are desirable. The genie of science could not be stuffed back into the bottle even if we so wished.

In theory, backward countries might still choose the simple life, but in practice they are clamoring for the devices and living standards of the West. The strongest appeal of Communist propaganda to retarded populations is in its promises of power dams, factories, mechanized farming, and the like. Much of the revolutionary leadership in Asia and Africa is provided by natives who have been educated in the West and have tasted its technological comforts and advantages.

Disparagement of the age of science and mass production, a nostalgia for the supposedly idyllic pre-scientific past, are familiar themes in twentieth-century literature. In 1954 a book titled *Tomorrow Is Already Here,* by Robert Jungk, warned that Americans are hell-bent for a soul-less, mechanized tomorrow, populated by dehumanized cogs in runaway machines.

I doubt whether those who denounce our world would, in the showdown, permanently exchange the material amenities of England, France, or America for those of darkest Africa. At the very least, I assume, they might spare the typewriters and printing presses with which they make themselves heard.

NOSTALGIA FOR WHAT?

As a cure for hatred of science, I recommend a protracted visit to some really primitive region of open sewers and open sores, cruel rates of infant mortality and decrepit old age at forty. Nostalgia for the simple past romanticizes drudgery, disease, and ignorance. It glosses over the poverty, social injustice, and feudal despotism that usually go along with a primitive economy.

The claim that there is an inherent conflict between science and our immortal souls—that science is the natural enemy of the soul—does not stand up under examination. The man in an airplane is not necessarily less devoted to truth, justice, and charity than his forefathers in oxcarts. Virtue does not necessarily go with primitive plumbing, and human dignity can be nurtured in a skyscraper no less than in a log cabin.

True, the marvels of technology have come upon us so suddenly that they have created problems of adjustment. Age-old inertias have been disturbed. But on the whole the adjustment has been remarkably good; the human problems caused by applied science are serious, but no more so than those it has solved. The crux of the matter is not in evils inseparable from technology but in the time lag in the assimilation of what technology has to offer.

MARX AND PROMETHEUS

The industrial revolution touched off by the steam engine brought trouble in its train: vile slums, child labor, brutal work hours and work conditions. But the time lag was bridged, slowly and surely. As capitalism matured, its fruits were spread to more and more people in goods, health, social security, and a new dignity of labor. Huge middle classes, not

23

foreseen by Karl Marx, have arisen. The distance between rich and poor, as measured by living standards, has steadily shrunk. The scientists who sparked the industrial revolution can rest in peace, their consciences assuaged.

The same, I believe, holds true of inventiveness in our own time, including the splitting of the atom. Every achievement on the physical plane packs danger as well as opportunity. It is the ancient dilemma posed when Prometheus gave man the fire that both warms and consumes. The inventive surge that brought us motorcars also made possible Panzer divisions. Pyromaniacs, however, cannot be blamed upon Prometheus, nor saturation bombing upon the Wright brothers.

It is well to recall that the twentieth century has also won victories, great and small, on the political, cultural, and moral levels. They are in evidence all around us, saturating our existence. They are spelled out in universal suffrage, civil freedoms, more widespread education, easier access to and greater appreciation of the products of genius in the arts; in society's growing acceptance of responsibility for the old, the widowed, the orphaned, and the helpless.

TECHNOLOGY AND THE SPIRIT

In my own lifetime I have seen the liberation of multitudes from overwork, exploitation, and ravaging diseases to which they had seemed forever condemned when I was a boy. It is not a worse but an immeasurably better society that we live in. The same decades that witnessed the control of the electron and the birth of nuclear energy also saw a substantial improvement in race and class relations and the enactment of vital social legislation. Along with the assembly line and automation has also come the rise of trade unions and a more equitable sharing of the products of labor and management.

America, the classic land of technology, enjoys the largest freedom from destitution, ignorance, and disease, along with political rights and social improvements unique in history. Its average citizen is not the common man but the uncommon man, for he has an amplitude of well-being and opportunity that pre-scientific societies reserved for a small and arrogant elite. Moreover—and this needs emphasis—the most magnificent flowering of science and technology has always occurred in countries where liberty prevailed. The close affinity between freedom and material abundance should give pause to those who derogate material progress.

"The figures show," Dr. Arthur H. Compton said recently, "that where technology has been used for the service of man, there is in broad total a healthy growth not only in man's biological life but also in his intellectual and spiritual life."

A society geared to technology is *compelled,* in order to remain viable, continually to lift the levels of human welfare. Greater purchasing power, more leisure, expanded relish for the end products of factories, communications, and entertainment—these are the very conditions of its survival. It draws its vitality from free men with an ever larger direct stake in the society, as totalitarians who would combine technology with slavery soon learn to their distress.

THE FINAL LINK

Science, far from nurturing pride, encourages humility. Its every victory reveals more clearly a Divine design in nature, a remarkable conformity in all things, from the infinitesimal to the infinite, that surpasses mortal understanding.

In its early stages, modern science seemed at odds with religion; but this was merely a token of its immaturity. The more familiar story, in our time, is that of scientists who become increasingly aware of the mystery of the universe and come to religion, in its fundamental sense, through knowledge of the limitations of science. And, indeed, how can those who play with the building blocks of the universe, its atoms and electrons and genes, fail to be touched by awe? More than ever, man's soul is involved in the equations of our lives.

Also the physical closeness engendered by science is promoting ever closer social and intellectual relations between peoples. Generations ago essential isolation of countries was taken for granted; it was a function of distance and difference. Today a dictatorship that would isolate its subjects must erect Iron Curtains and walls of electronic jamming. With worldwide television, which I regard as a certainty before 1980, the sense of our common humanity will deepen. It is the strange, the unknown, that frightens—but the strangeness will be removed by visual contact, to reveal the familiar physiognomy of our neighbors.

We know in our hearts that modern war can cause such overwhelming devastation to life and property as to become a species of suicide. The atom and the electron have made it almost as disastrous for the winner as for the loser. This decisive fact must, in the long run, cancel out war as an instrument of national policy. We cannot know when or what form the coming "one world" will take, but world law enforced by world police seems inherent in the age of science and technology.

The forces I have discussed appear to me to cause a chain reaction. First, science and technology create material abundance. Second, this produces new conditions and demands that compel adjustments with resulting social advances. Third, the interdependence of people in a world shrunk by science inevitably requires broader mental concepts, which lead to greater ethical and moral stature—which in turn stimulate man's spiritual growth.

It seems to me unqualifiedly good that more and more of the weight of arduous toil will be unloaded onto the backs of machines; that the sum total of pain and agony will be further reduced by the progress of healing; that modern communications will bring peoples and nations into closer contact, leading to better understanding of one another.

3   The Challenge of Communism

The next twenty-five years, however, will be marked by great challenges to our courage, character, wisdom, and stamina. The greatest of these challenges, of course, will be the continuing Communist drive for world dominion.

The pendulum of Soviet diplomacy has swung between "tough" and "tame," depending on the Kremlin's need for time, the domestic situation in Russia, etc. At this writing Soviet policy appears to be veering toward the "tame" end of the curve. But the essence of Kremlin policy, as defined by its leaders from Lenin on, has never changed. One must hope, therefore, that the free world has learned at last not to drop its guard under the spell of the Kremlin's tactical amiability. Even if the Soviets should agree to "call off the cold war," it will not end the danger—the Communists have not been celebrated for keeping their pledges.

NEEDED: A "CRASH PROGRAM"

Our overriding duty, in the years ahead, will be to make it crystal clear that the outcome of war, if the Soviets provoke a final showdown, will be far from assured. We must generate and maintain enough military vitality to convince the Kremlin that an attack on us would be a suicidal gamble for them. Whatever else we may do in the next quarter-century to reduce and in time remove the Soviet menace, it will be futile unless backed by adequate military force both offensive and defensive, conventional and atomic.

On the side of the offensive, the means of *delivering* destruction have become far more important than the means of destruction. In the H-bomb we have reached the ultimate in militarily useful explosive power; bigger bombs would be meaningless. Beyond this point the decisive elements in the equation will be range, speed, and accuracy in placing the explosives on the target.

This compels us to focus brains and energy on long-range bombers capable of fighting their way to the objective. It demands—and this seems to me the most important immediate need—clear superiority in the development of the longest-range guided projectiles, the so-called IBM or Intercontinental Ballistic Missile. A "crash program" to assure such superiority is called for. At the same time, especially while we are forging the new weapons of conflict in the third dimension, we must maintain our ground and sea forces at adequate levels.

But defensive vitality is no less important. The widespread idea that "defense has become impossible" is unwarranted and dangerous. Those who proclaim it usually mean that *complete* defense is not possible; but that is a truism, since there never has been a defense that could not be breached. True, a breakthrough today, in nuclear terms, can mean disastrous damage. But that is no excuse for failure to make all possible defensive preparations for the coming quarter-century.

The certainty that an attacker would suffer large-scale attrition—that he would sacrifice many planes and missiles for the one that gets through—would be powerful reinforcement for the deterrent value of our offensive strength.

Methods of electronic detection of planes and missiles are known. So are techniques for destroying them through automatic ground-to-air and air-to-air collision. In the defensive areas, what is involved is primarily an electronic contest. And in that, we have every reason to believe, the U. S. enjoys the substantial advantages that flow from its present technological superiority—in terms of resources, inventiveness, experience, and national skills.

COUNTERMEASURES ARE VITAL

The immediate danger is not a bombing contest but the debilitating, bankrupting, ruthless, and relentless Communist offensive in a cold war that may continue throughout the coming quarter-century. Until the advent of the Soviet regime, nations were either at peace or at war. Consequently they find it hard today to adjust their thinking and policies to a condition that is neither one nor the other in the traditional sense. We do not shrink from appropriating $50 billion or even more for armaments, but we are still reluctant to spend a few billions to meet the more urgent needs of the prevailing cold war.

Because there is no sound of shooting, no thunder of exploding bombs, we do not as yet have the feeling of life-and-death urgency. But it *is* that urgent. Our defeat in the present nonmilitary struggle would doom what remains of freedom on this planet as completely as defeat in a shooting war.

The cold war is where the *Communists* are determined to defeat *us.* And that, by the same token, is where *we* could defeat *them,* once we recognized the new state of affairs and decided to meet it resolutely, with the same concentration of effort, the same readiness for sacrifice and risk, the same dedication to victory as if it were an old-style military challenge.

The West and its allies in Asia can capture the initiative

only by a definite decision: to win the cold war, or at the very least to prevent the Communists from winning it. In my view, this is the only real guarantee against a hot war.

The question, in truth, is not *whether* we should engage in political, economic, and psychological warfare, the principal weapons used in the cold war. The Soviets have driven us to take nonmilitary countermeasures of some sort. But these have been piecemeal, uncoordinated, and on a pitifully inadequate scale. The question, rather, is whether we should turn their own political and psychological weapons against the Communists with a clearheaded determination to make our counteroffensive truly effective in the quarter-century ahead.

The job is global in size. Local problems by the score will have to be solved as they arise. But these can be solved if they are subordinated to an over-all strategy geared to victory. The magnitude of the commitment and its colossal stakes call for focused planning and direction. We need a strategic High Command in this vital area analogous to the Joint Chiefs of Staff in the military area. And our efforts must be continually coordinated with the agencies of cold warfare in other free countries.

The Soviet orbit is vulnerable to political and psychological weapons. The Kremlin knows this well and fears it most. Its internal "contradictions" are much sharper than those in the free world. The tensions between Soviet Russia and the satellite peoples are enormous—we saw some of them snap in Germany, Czechoslovakia, and Poland in June, 1953.

Popular discontent inside Soviet Russia itself is widespread. After thirty-eight years of absolute power, the Kremlin does not yet dare to taper off its use of raw force—political arrests by the million, large-scale executions, continuous purges, and total suppression of elementary human rights.

Fear of its own subjects, doubts about their allegiance in time of crisis, are chronic in the Kremlin.

PROGRESS OR SAVAGERY?

The importance of winning the cold war cannot be glossed over in looking ahead to 1980. Unless we assure peace, unless we gain the initiative in the cold conflict—by means short of hot war—the triumphs of science and technology that I have sketched in broad strokes will be emptied of meaning.

If freedom is lost, if the dignity of man is destroyed, advances on the material plane will not be "progress" but a foundation for a new savagery. Mankind cannot indefinitely carry the mounting burdens of an armaments race, and the greater burdens of fear and uncertainty. Our supreme commitment, as we look ahead to a crucial quarter-century, must be to win the peace—not a peace of totalitarian dominion but a genuine peace rooted in liberty. I believe it can be done.

JOHN VON NEUMANN
Member, Atomic Energy Commission

Budapest-born John von Neumann, like many fellow scientists of the atomic age, harbors a streak of the blues but his delicate shade may be called constructive pessimism. It does not hamper creativity. One von Neumann creation, the mathematical and numerical integrator and calculator (often called MANIAC), played a key role in building the H-bomb, and has also produced new meteorological understanding that may aid climate control. Dr. von Neumann is also celebrated for his pathbreaking study of strategy in poker, business, and war (*Theory of Games and Economic Behavior,* written with Oskar Morgenstern). Dr. von Neumann joined the Institute for Advanced Study at Princeton in 1933, four years before he was naturalized, and took leave after President Eisenhower appointed him to the AEC. Born in 1903, he studied engineering and mathematics in Europe. Since 1940 he has been a consultant to the U.S. armed forces, and for contributions to Los Alamos and similar projects he has won two major U.S. decorations.

Can We Survive Technology?

BY JOHN VON NEUMANN

"The great globe itself" is in a rapidly maturing crisis—a crisis attributable to the fact that the environment in which technological progress must occur has become both under-sized and underorganized. To define the crisis with any accuracy, and to explore possibilities of dealing with it, we must not only look at relevant facts, but also engage in some speculation. The process will illuminate some potential technological developments of the next quarter-century.

In the first half of this century the accelerating industrial revolution encountered an absolute limitation—not on technological progress as such but on an essential safety factor. This safety factor, which had permitted the industrial revolution to roll on from the mid-eighteenth to the early twentieth century, was essentially a matter of geographical and political *Lebensraum:* an ever broader geographical scope for technological activities, combined with an ever broader political integration of the world. Within this expanding framework it was possible to accommodate the major tensions created by technological progress.

Now this safety mechanism is being sharply inhibited; literally and figuratively, we are running out of room. At long last, we begin to feel the effects of the finite, actual size of the earth in a critical way.

Thus the crisis does not arise from accidental events or human errors. It is inherent in technology's relation to geography on the one hand and to political organization on the other. The crisis was developing visibly in the 1940's, and some phases can be traced back to 1914. In the years between now and 1980 the crisis will probably develop far beyond all earlier patterns. When or how it will end—or to what state of affairs it will yield—nobody can say.

DANGERS—PRESENT AND COMING

In all its stages the industrial revolution consisted of making available more and cheaper energy, more and easier controls of human actions and reactions, and more and faster communications. Each development increased the effectiveness of the other two. All three factors increased the speed of performing large-scale operations—industrial, mercantile, political, and migratory. But throughout the development, increased speed did not so much shorten time requirements of processes as extend the areas of the earth affected by them. The reason is clear. Since most *time* scales are fixed by human reaction times, habits, and other physiological and psychological factors, the effect of the increased speed of technological processes was to enlarge the *size* of units—political, organizational, economic, and cultural—affected by technological operations. That is, instead of performing the same operations as before in less time, now larger-scale operations were performed in the same time. This important evolution has a natural limit, that of the earth's actual size. The limit is now being reached, or at least closely approached.

Indications of this appeared early and with dramatic force in the military sphere. By 1940 even the larger countries of continental Western Europe were inadequate as military units. Only Russia could sustain a major military reverse without collapsing. Since 1945, improved aeronautics and communications alone might have sufficed to make any geographical unit, including Russia, inadequate in a future war. The advent of nuclear weapons merely climaxes the development. Now the effectiveness of offensive weapons is such as to stultify all plausible defensive time scales. As early as World War I, it was observed that the admiral commanding the battle fleet could "lose the British Empire in one afternoon." Yet navies of that epoch were relatively stable entities, tolerably safe against technological surprises. Today there is every reason to fear that even minor inventions and feints in the field of nuclear weapons can be decisive in less time than would be required to devise specific countermeasures. Soon existing nations will be as unstable in war as a nation the size of Manhattan Island would have been in a contest fought with the weapons of 1900.

Such military instability has already found its political expression. Two superpowers, the U.S. and U.S.S.R., represent such enormous destructive potentials as to afford little chance of a purely passive equilibrium. Other countries, including possible "neutrals," are militarily defenseless in the ordinary sense. At best they will acquire destructive capabilities of their own, as Britain is now doing. Consequently, the "concert of powers"—or its equivalent international organization —rests on a basis much more fragile than ever before. The situation is further embroiled by the newly achieved political effectiveness of non-European nationalisms.

These factors would "normally"—that is, in any recent century—have led to war. Will they lead to war before 1980? Or soon thereafter? It would be presumptuous to try to answer such a question firmly. In any case, the present and the near future are both dangerous. While the immediate problem is to cope with the actual danger, it is also essential to envisage how the problem is going to evolve in the 1955–80 period, even assuming that all will go reasonably well for the moment. This does not mean belittling immediate problems of weaponry, of U.S.-U.S.S.R. tensions, of the evolution and revolutions of Asia. These first things must come first. But we must be ready for the follow-up, lest possible immediate successes prove futile. We must think beyond the present forms of problems to those of later decades.

WHEN REACTORS GROW UP

Technological evolution is still accelerating. Technologies are always constructive and beneficial, directly or indirectly. Yet their consequences tend to increase instability—a point that will get closer attention after we have had a look at certain aspects of continuing technological evolution.

First of all, there is a rapidly expanding supply of energy. It is generally agreed that even conventional, chemical fuel—coal or oil—will be available in increased quantity in the next two decades. Increasing demand tends to keep fuel prices high, yet improvements in methods of generation seem to bring the price of power down. There is little doubt that the most significant event affecting energy is the advent of nuclear power. Its only available controlled source today is the nuclear-fission reactor. Reactor techniques appear to be approaching a condition in which they will be competitive with conventional (chemical) power sources within the U.S.; however, because of generally higher fuel prices abroad, they could already be more than competitive in many important foreign areas. Yet reactor technology is but a decade and a half old, during most of which period effort has been directed primarily not toward power but toward plutonium production. Given a decade of really large-scale industrial effort, the economic characteristics of reactors will undoubtedly surpass those of the present by far.

Moreover, it is not a law of nature that all controlled release of nuclear energy should be tied to fission reactions as it has been thus far. It is true that nuclear energy appears to be the primary source of practically all energy now visible in nature. Furthermore, it is not surprising that the first break into the intranuclear domain occurred at the unstable "high end" of the system of nuclei (that is, by fission). Yet fission is not nature's normal way of releasing nuclear energy. In the long run, systematic industrial exploitation of nuclear energy may shift reliance onto other and still more abundant modes. Again, reactors have been bound thus far to the traditional heat-steam-generator-electricity cycle, just as automobiles were at first constructed to look like buggies. It is likely that we shall gradually develop procedures more naturally and effectively adjusted to the new source of energy, abandoning the conventional kinks and detours inherited from chemical-fuel processes. Consequently, a few decades hence energy may be free—just like the unmetered air—with coal and oil used mainly as raw materials for organic chemical synthesis, to which, as experience has shown, their properties are best suited.

"ALCHEMY" AND AUTOMATION

It is worth emphasizing that the main trend will be systematic exploration of nuclear reactions—that is, the transmutation of elements, or alchemy rather than chemistry. The main point in developing the industrial use of nuclear processes is to make them suitable for large-scale exploitation on the relatively small site that is the earth or, rather, any plausible terrestrial industrial establishment. Nature has, of course, been operating nuclear processes all along, well and massively, but her "natural" sites for this industry are entire stars. There is reason to believe that the minimum space requirements for her way of operating are the minimum sizes of stars. Forced by the limitations of our real estate, we must in this respect do much better than nature. That this may not be impossible has been demonstrated in the somewhat extreme and unnatural instance of fission, that remarkable breakthrough of the past decade.

What massive transmutation of elements will do to technology in general is hard to imagine, but the effects will be radical indeed. This can already be sensed in related fields. The general revolution clearly under way in the military sphere, and its already realized special aspect, the terrible possibilities of mass destruction, should not be viewed as typical of what the nuclear revolution stands for. Yet they may well be typical of how deeply that revolution will transform whatever it touches. And the revolution will probably touch most things technological.

Also likely to evolve fast—and quite apart from nuclear evolution—is automation. Interesting analyses of recent developments in this field, and of near-future potentialities, have appeared in the last few years. Automatic control, of course, is as old as the industrial revolution, for the decisive new feature of Watt's steam engine was its automatic valve control, including speed control by a "governor." In our century, however, small electric amplifying and switching devices put automation on an entirely new footing. This development began with the electromechanical (telephone) relay, continued and unfolded with the vacuum tube, and appears to accelerate with various solid-state devices (semiconductor crystals, ferromagnetic cores, etc.). The last decade or two has also witnessed an increasing ability to control and "discipline" large numbers of such devices within one machine. Even in an airplane the number of vacuum tubes now approaches or exceeds a thousand. Other machines, containing up to 10,000 vacuum tubes, up to five times more crystals, and possibly more than 100,000 cores, now operate faultlessly over long periods, performing many millions of regulated, preplanned actions per second, with an expectation of only a few errors per day or week.

Many such machines have been built to perform complicated scientific and engineering calculations and large-scale accounting and logistical surveys. There is no doubt that they will be used for elaborate industrial process control, logistical, economic, and other planning, and many other purposes heretofore lying entirely outside the compass of quantitative and automatic control and preplanning. Thanks to simplified forms of automatic or semi-automatic control, the efficiency of some important branches of industry has increased considerably during recent decades. It is therefore to be expected that the considerably elaborated newer forms, now becoming increasingly available, will effect much more along these lines.

Fundamentally, improvements in control are really improvements in communicating information within an organization or mechanism. The sum total of progress in this sphere is explosive. Improvements in communication in its direct, physical sense—transportation—while less dramatic, have been considerable and steady. If nuclear developments make energy unrestrictedly available, transportation developments are likely to accelerate even more. But even "normal" progress in sea, land, and air media is extremely important. Just such "normal" progress molded the world's economic development, producing the present global ideas in politics and economics.

CONTROLLED CLIMATE

Let us now consider a thoroughly "abnormal" industry and its potentialities—that is, an industry as yet without a place in any list of major activities: the control of weather or, to use a more ambitious but justified term, climate. One phase of this activity that has received a good deal of public attention is "rain making." The present technique assumes extensive rain clouds, and forces precipitation by applying small amounts of chemical agents. While it is not easy to evaluate the significance of the efforts made thus far, the evidence seems to indicate that the aim is an attainable one.

But weather control and climate control are really much broader than rain making. All major weather phenomena, as well as climate as such, are ultimately controlled by the solar energy that falls on the earth. To modify the amount of solar energy, is, of course, beyond human power. But what really matters is not the amount that hits the earth, but the fraction retained by the earth, since that reflected back into space is no more useful than if it had never arrived. Now, the amount absorbed by the solid earth, the sea, or the atmosphere seems to be subject to delicate influences. True, none of these has so far been substantially controlled by human will, but there are strong indications of control possibilities.

The carbon dioxide released into the atmosphere by industry's burning of coal and oil—more than half of it during the last generation—may have changed the atmosphere's composition sufficiently to account for a general warming of the world by about one degree Fahrenheit. The volcano Krakatao erupted in 1883 and released an amount of energy by no means exorbitant. Had the dust of the eruption stayed in the stratosphere for fifteen years, reflecting sunlight away from the earth, it might have sufficed to lower the world's temperature by six degrees (in fact, it stayed for about three years, and five such eruptions would probably have achieved the result mentioned). This would have been a substantial cooling; the last Ice Age, when half of North America and all of northern and western Europe were under an ice cap like that of Greenland or Antarctica, was only fifteen degrees colder than the present age. On the other hand, another fifteen degrees of warming would probably melt the ice of Greenland and Antarctica and produce worldwide tropical to semi-tropical climate.

"RATHER FANTASTIC EFFECTS"

Furthermore, it is known that the persistence of large ice fields is due to the fact that ice both reflects sunlight energy and radiates away terrestrial energy at an even higher rate than ordinary soil. Microscopic layers of colored matter spread on an icy surface, or in the atmosphere above one, could inhibit the reflection-radiation process, melt the ice, and change the local climate. Measures that would effect such changes are technically possible, and the amount of investment required would be only of the order of magnitude that sufficed to develop rail systems and other major industries. The main difficulty lies in predicting in detail the effects of any such drastic intervention. But our knowledge of the dynamics and the controlling processes in the atmosphere is rapidly approaching a level that would permit such prediction. Probably intervention in atmospheric and climatic matters will come in a few decades, and will unfold on a scale difficult to imagine at present.

What could be done, of course, is no index to what should be done; to make a new ice age in order to annoy others, or a new tropical, "interglacial" age in order to please everybody, is not necessarily a rational program. In fact, to evaluate the ultimate consequences of either a general cooling or a general heating would be a complex matter. Changes would affect the level of the seas, and hence the habitability of the continental coastal shelves; the evaporation of the seas, and hence general precipitation and glaciation levels; and so on. What would be harmful and what beneficial—and to which regions of the earth—is not immediately obvious. But there is little doubt that one *could* carry out analyses needed to predict results, intervene on any desired scale, and ultimately achieve rather fantastic effects. The climate of specific regions and levels of precipitation might be altered. For example, temporary disturbances—including invasions of cold (polar) air that constitute the typical winter of the middle latitudes, and tropical storms (hurricanes)—might be corrected or at least depressed.

There is no need to detail what such things would mean to agriculture or, indeed, to all phases of human, animal, and plant ecology. What power over our environment, over all nature, is implied!

Such actions would be more directly and truly worldwide than recent or, presumably, future wars, or than the economy at any time. Extensive human intervention would deeply affect the atmosphere's general circulation, which depends on the earth's rotation and intensive solar heating of the tropics. Measures in the arctic may control the weather in temperate regions, or measures in one temperate region critically affect another, one-quarter around the globe. All this will merge each nation's affairs with those of every other, more thoroughly than the threat of a nuclear or any other war may already have done.

THE INDIFFERENT CONTROLS

Such developments as free energy, greater automation, improved communications, partial or total climate control, have common traits deserving special mention. First, though all are intrinsically useful, they can lend themselves to destruction. Even the most formidable tools of nuclear destruction are only extreme members of a genus that includes useful methods of energy release or element transmutation. The most constructive schemes for climate control would have to be based on insights and techniques that would also lend themselves to forms of climatic warfare as yet unimagined. Technology—like science—is neutral all through, providing only means of control applicable to any purpose, indifferent to all.

Second, there is in most of these developments a trend toward affecting the earth as a whole, or to be more exact, toward producing effects that can be projected from any one to any other point on the earth. There is an intrinsic conflict with geography—and institutions based thereon—as understood today. Of course, any technology interacts with geography, and each imposes its own geographical rules and modalities. The technology that is now developing and that will dominate the next decades seems to be in total conflict with traditional and, in the main, momentarily still valid, geographical and political units and concepts. This is the maturing crisis of technology.

What kind of action does this situation call for? *Whatever* one feels inclined to do, one decisive trait must be considered: the very techniques that create the dangers and the instabilities are in themselves useful, or closely related to the useful. In fact, the more useful they could be, the more unstabilizing their effects can also be. It is not a particular perverse destructiveness of one particular invention that creates danger. Technological power, technological efficiency as such, is an ambivalent achievement. Its danger is intrinsic.

SCIENCE THE INDIVISIBLE

In looking for a solution, it is well to exclude one pseudo-solution at the start. The crisis will not be resolved by inhibiting this or that apparently particularly obnoxious form of technology. For one thing, the parts of technology, as well as of the underlying sciences, are so intertwined that in the long run nothing less than a total elimination of all technological

43

progress would suffice for inhibition. Also, on a more pedestrian and immediate basis, useful and harmful techniques lie everywhere so close together that it is never possible to separate the lions from the lambs. This is known to all who have so laboriously tried to separate secret, "classified" science or technology (military) from the "open" kind; success is never more—nor intended to be more—than transient, lasting perhaps half a decade. Similarly, a separation into useful and harmful subjects in any technological sphere would probably diffuse into nothing in a decade.

Moreover, in this case successful separation would have to be enduring (unlike the case of military "classification," in which even a few years' gain may be important). Also, the proximity of useful techniques to harmful ones, and the possibility of putting the harmful ones to military use, puts a competitive premium on infringement. Hence the banning of particular technologies would have to be enforced on a worldwide basis. But the only authority that could do this effectively would have to be of such scope and perfection as to signal the *resolution* of international problems rather than the discovery of a *means* to resolve them.

Finally and, I believe, most importantly, prohibition of technology (invention and development, which are hardly separable from underlying scientific inquiry) is contrary to the whole ethos of the industrial age. It is irreconcilable with a major mode of intellectuality as our age understands it. It is hard to imagine such a restraint successfully imposed in our civilization. Only if those disasters that we fear had already occurred, only if humanity were already completely disillusioned about technological civilization, could such a step be taken. But not even the disasters of recent wars have produced that degree of disillusionment, as is proved by the phenomenal resiliency with which the industrial way of life recovered even—or particularly—in the worst-hit areas. The technological system retains enormous vitality, probably more than ever before, and the counsel of restraint is unlikely to be heeded.

SURVIVAL—A POSSIBILITY

A much more satisfactory solution than technological prohibition would be eliminating war as "a means of national policy." The desire to do this is as old as any part of the ethical system by which we profess to be governed. The intensity of the sentiment fluctuates, increasing greatly after major wars. How strong is it now and is it on the up or the downgrade? It is certainly strong, for practical as well as for emotional reasons, all quite obvious. At least in individuals, it seems worldwide, transcending differences of political systems. Yet in evaluating its durability and effectiveness a certain caution is justified.

One can hardly quarrel with the "practical" arguments against war, but the emotional factors are probably less stable. Memories of the 1939–45 war are fresh, but it is not easy to estimate what will happen to popular sentiment as they recede. The revulsion that followed 1914–18 did not stand up twenty years later under the strain of a serious political crisis. The elements of a future international conflict are clearly present today and even more explicit than after 1914–18. Whether the "practical" considerations, without the emotional counterpart, will suffice to restrain the human species is dubious since the past record is so spotty. True, "practical" reasons are stronger than ever before, since war could be vastly more destructive than formerly. But that very *appearance* has been observed several times in the past without being decisive. True, this time the danger of destruction seems to be real rather than apparent, but there is no guarantee that a real danger can

45

control human actions better than a convincing appearance of danger.

What safeguard remains? Apparently only day-to-day—or perhaps year-to-year—opportunistic measures, a long sequence of small, correct decisions. And this is not surprising. After all, the crisis is due to the rapidity of progress, to the probable further acceleration thereof, and to the reaching of certain critical relationships. Specifically, the effects that we are now beginning to produce are of the same order of magnitude as that of "the great globe itself." Indeed, they affect the earth as an entity. Hence further acceleration can no longer be absorbed as in the past by an extension of the area of operations. Under present conditions it is unreasonable to expect a novel cure-all.

For progress there is no cure. Any attempt to find automatically safe channels for the present explosive variety of progress must lead to frustration. The only safety possible is relative, and it lies in an intelligent exercise of day-to-day judgment.

AWFUL AND MORE AWFUL

The problems created by the combination of the presently possible forms of nuclear warfare and the rather unusually unstable international situation are formidable and not to be solved easily. Those of the next decades are likely to be similarly vexing, "only more so." The U.S.-U.S.S.R. tension is bad, but when other nations begin to make felt their full offensive potential weight, things will not become simpler.

Present awful possibilities of nuclear warfare may give way to others even more awful. After global climate control becomes possible, perhaps all our present involvements will seem simple. We should not deceive ourselves: once such possibilities become actual, they will be exploited. It will, therefore, be necessary to develop suitable new political forms and procedures. All experience shows that even smaller technological changes than those now in the cards profoundly transform political and social relationships. Experience also shows that these transformations are not *a priori* predictable and that most contemporary "first guesses" concerning them are wrong. For all these reasons, one should take neither present difficulties nor presently proposed reforms too seriously.

The one solid fact is that the difficulties are due to an evolution that, while useful and constructive, is also dangerous. Can we produce the required adjustments with the necessary speed? The most hopeful answer is that the human species has been subjected to similar tests before and seems to have a congenital ability to come through, after varying amounts of trouble. To ask in advance for a complete recipe would be unreasonable. We can specify only the human qualities required: patience, flexibility, intelligence.

GEORGE MEANY

President, AFL-CIO

George Meany is head of the largest free labor organization in the world, and is perhaps the most important individual shaping U.S. labor's thoughts today. The U.S. labor movement, once considered "backward" by its Marxist critics, is today a model for European and Asiatic movements. The growth of organized labor from a membership of under two million, twenty-five years ago, to its enormous power and prestige today is itself one of the significant features of the modern free-enterprise system. It is unlikely that labor will grow at any comparable rate in the next twenty-five years, but certainly it will not diminish. Its economic demands and its political thinking will affect the nature of American capitalism in the next twenty-five years as profoundly as they have done in the past quarter-century.

What Labor Means by "More"

BY GEORGE MEANY

To put aside the pressing problems of the day and to speculate about the America of 1980 is a challenging exercise of the
imagination. Given the fabulous inventiveness of our country,
and the promises of technology, the America of 1980 might
be even more unrecognizable to us today than is the America
of twenty-five years ago. But without world peace as a foundation of the future, rational predictions about the next quarter-
century are utterly impossible. Moreover, advances in technology alone do not and cannot solve the great questions of social
arrangements and social justice. These are questions not of
technology but of morals, not of science but of wisdom.

Plain realism dictates, therefore, that our thinking about
the America of the quarter-century ahead must be limited to
goals rather than to predictions. Yet long-range goals, if they
are meaningful, originate in the world of today, and are shaped
by one's tradition, and one's philosophy. In a single man's
lifetime, twenty-five years is a long time, perhaps half the span
of his mature, vigorous life. Institutions, and the men who reflect them, have a longer perspective than individuals alone,
and in the A.F. of L.* our traditions and our philosophy have
emerged from an experience of seventy-five years. Our goals

---

* *Mr. Meany's paper was written prior to the recent merger of the A.F. of
L. and the C.I.O. and his own elevation to the presidency of the combined
organizations.*—EDITORS.

can be understood only in terms of that experience. Moreover, the goals of a future but a quarter of a century away will not appear so unreal when measured against a philosophy hammered out by millions of Americans over the course of three-quarters of a century.

Our goals as trade-unionists are modest, for we do not seek to recast American society in any particular doctrinaire or ideological image. We seek an ever rising standard of living. Sam Gompers once put the matter succinctly. When asked what the labor movement wanted, he answered "More." If by a better standard of living we mean not only more money but more leisure and a richer cultural life, the answer remains, "More."

But how do we get "more"? Imperfect in many details as our system may be, this country has adopted a flexible method for increasing the standard of living while maintaining freedom. It is the method of voluntary collective bargaining, of free decision-making outside the coercions of government, in the solution of economic disagreement. And it is through the give-and-take of collective bargaining that we seek to achieve our goals.

WHEN FREE MEN BARGAIN . . .

Collective bargaining, we have learned, can exist only in the environment of political freedom. Where there is no individual liberty, there is no free trade-union movement either. Every dictator, from left to right, as a first step in the consolidation of power has sought to destroy free trade unions. And so we are dedicated to freedom, not only political but also economic, through a system of private enterprise. We believe in the American profit system. We believe in free competition. The American private-enterprise system, despite some defects, has achieved far greater results for wage earners than any other social system in history. The American worker, without doubt, is the best-paid, best-clothed, and best-housed worker in the world. But he can and should be much better paid, better clothed, and better housed in 1980. The children of American workers have greater educational opportunities than children of any other workers; the workers' wives and families have greater comforts and opportunities for social and cultural development than families of workers in any other land. These comforts and opportunities, too, can be greatly increased over the next quarter-century.

We are proud, understandably, of the contribution of trade-unionism to the changing American private-enterprise system. Certainly we have differed with our employers over the sharing of the benefits—this is the heart of bargaining—and we shall differ again during the next quarter-century. But throughout we have relied upon the judgment of free men, unimpeded by the interference of government, to reach private agreement, and it is certainly the hope and resolve of the A.F. of L. that our differences shall continue to be settled in this way.

On its philosophical side, collective bargaining is a means of assuring justice and fair treatment. In the economic realm it is a means of prodding management to increase efficiency and output, and of placing upon trade unions great responsibilities to limit their demands to practical realities. A failure to recognize the unique role of collective bargaining is a failure to understand the distinctive new nature of American private enterprise as it has evolved over the past seventy-five years.

THE RIGHTS OF MANAGEMENT

Are we likely, by 1980, to reach the limits of collective bargaining? For the A.F. of L., I can say flatly that collective

51

bargaining is not a means of seeking a voice in management. We do not want so-called "codetermination"—the representation of unions on the board of directors or in the active management of a company. In Germany, where trade unions have endorsed such a plan, codetermination emerges from a peculiar background—the political use of corporate power by cartel management. And in that country it has some logic as a means of maintaining economic democracy. Here in the U.S., with a different background and tradition, with a different kind of management, with the acceptance of collective bargaining, codetermination has no reality. To some in management, any limitation of management's right to set the conditions of work is a challenge to its integrity. But this point of view is diminishing. I would expect that by 1980 it will have disappeared completely.

There remains the more concrete and difficult question of where a line can be drawn. In recent years certainly the scope of collective bargaining has expanded considerably. Where once it included largely wages, hours, and maintenance of health and safety conditions, and, later, hiring, firing, and promotion, it now includes medical care, pensions, and the like. Today labor is beginning to question the unilateral right of management to set production standards and even (as in the recent hatters' strike in Norwalk, Connecticut) to stipulate the location of plant.

While exact answers are hard to give, a general principle can be established: A union exists to protect the livelihood and interests of a worker. Those matters that do not touch a worker directly, a union cannot and will not challenge. These may include investment policy, a decision to make a new product, a desire to erect a new plant so as to be closer to expanding markets, to re-invest out of earnings or seek new equity capital, etc. But where management decisions affect a worker directly, a union will intervene. When a company, for example, renounces union standards, and arbitrarily disrupts the lives of thousands of workers because it may save 7 cents a hat, a union will resist. If trade unions in 1980 are not willing to resist such efforts, they will not have—and would not deserve—the kind of influence they hold in the U.S. in 1955.

Merely because management bears the responsibility of managing, it does not acquire the right to pay less than a decent wage as a condition of staying in business. Nor does an effective management allow its plant to become run-down and antiquated. Workers should not bear the price of management's errors. Lincoln once put it: "Labor is prior to and independent of capital. Capital is only the fruit of labor, and could not have existed if labor had not first existed. Labor is the superior of capital and deserves much the higher consideration. . . ."

THAT YEAR-ROUND WAGE

In the next twenty-five years the form of collective bargaining will, as in the past, adjust to the changing structure and functioning of business itself. The type of collective bargaining that is practical for a small, local employer is not suitable for a national, multiplant employer. The economics of the industry, the structure of the enterprise, and the scope of union recognition are the principal factors dictating the type of collective bargaining. The A.F. of L. has not been rigid or static. In the atomic-energy field, for example, where a multiplicity of crafts creates bargaining problems, the A.F. of L. has evolved a new form whereby craft workers are free to choose their own union, but bargaining is conducted through a joint council. The A.F. of L. machinists in organizing aircraft, or the teamsters in organizing distribution workers, have evolved new union forms to provide efficient service to their members and effective power in bargaining.

Industry today is moving toward decentralization of plant. In the next twenty-five years decentralization probably will be a prime feature of corporate decision-making and corporate management. Inevitably, collective bargaining will have to be adapted to the changing nature of managerial patterns. But collective bargaining is no mere reflex to industrial change. Where firms decentralize in order to move into low-wage areas, or to break up existing wage structures, unions will not acquiesce. Bargaining follows the fact not the form of management. One bargains where there is effective power.

Not only the forms of bargaining but the range of issues are subject to change and modification. At the moment, regularity of income or of consuming power is being sought by some unions through a guaranteed annual wage. Actually, the goal is not new; it is simply one more projection of the basic desire of workers for a decent year-round standard of living. Perhaps "guaranteed" is a misnomer, subject to misinterpretation. Few things in the world can be "guaranteed." But a worker wants to "regularize" his pay and assure himself a year-round income so that he can plan and pay for his purchases. And this objective has been sought in different ways according to the different characters of industries. For example, the apparently high hourly rate of pay earned in the building-and-construction industry is a device enabling a worker and his family to live during the industry's annual "off season." This is true also in other industries where there is a large seasonal variation or a high degree of transiency among workers. Thus while the guaranteed annual wage is a good objective, the nature of the industry limits its application, and in some industries it is highly impractical. We hope, however, that by 1980 we shall be able to expand our economy in orderly fashion so that the guarantee of year-round incomes for all workers is no longer a problem.

WHO'S AFRAID OF AUTOMATION?

In the next twenty-five years the flexibility of collective bargaining will meet its severest test in the rapid changes in the technological structure of industry and the consequent wholesale changes in the character of the labor force. This problem is symbolized by the term automation. By 1980 we may have completely "automatic" factories, run by electronically set devices without the intervention of human hand. But we know from experience that progress in technology does not occur in large, magical jumps, but grows out of past advances. Similarly, the attendant problems of adapting to progress do not change basically; they simply appear larger and more complex. Our concern, thus, is less with 1980 than with the road to it.

Certainly the trade-union movement does not oppose technological change. There can be no turning back to a negative or shortsighted policy of limiting progress. (During the depression someone half seriously proposed a five-year moratorium on new inventions.) The answer to technological change lies in smoothing its transitions and cushioning the shocks that attend it. This means, in the immediate sense, the establishment of severance pay, retraining of skills, reorganization of work schedules. These are social costs that industry will have to bear in order to avoid the wasting of human resources—and to avoid our calling on government to bear these costs if industry fails to do so.

In the longer run we shall press for the time-proved policy of reduction of hours. Through shortened hours, workers not only have more leisure but we are able to "spread the work." We have set our sights on a thirty-hour week. By 1980 that should be easily attainable for all Americans.

In view of the American productive achievement, the proposal cannot be brushed aside by present-day pessimists. Years ago, when organized labor first proposed a reduction in hours, reactionary interests said it would not work. But it has worked. There are more persons at work today, not at ten hours a day six days a week, but eight hours a day five days a week, than at any time before. Since the beginning of the century the standard of living in the U.S. has doubled, although working hours average nearly 33 per cent less than in 1900. There is no reason why this achievement cannot be repeated by 1980.

The decision to keep the level of consumption even with the development of production is in the hands of men, not of "market forces," or the blind operation of so-called laws of economics. The decisions are man-made and can be shaped by the cooperative efforts of unions and management. We must not wait until millions are unemployed and human resources have gone to waste. Prompt and sensible action is necessary now.

THE HAND OF GOVERNMENT

The A.F. of L. is primarily an economic organization, seeking its ends in the economic field. In recent years we have been involved with government. Whether we shall continue to be so involved in the next twenty-five years depends in large measure on industry. Only when industry has failed to accept social responsibility has labor, along with the people as a whole, turned to government for help. There is always the danger that concentration of power may whittle away individual freedoms. In fact, the heavy hand of government in the past has throttled freedom for private collective bargaining perhaps more than it throttled freedom for private enterprise. But government has an obligation to help people do what they cannot do for themselves.

What Labor Means by "More"

The A.F. of L., for example, at one time opposed a government system of social security. We felt that through private collective bargaining wages could be raised high enough for the individual to accumulate his own savings, or pay for his own annuity, thus assuring himself security. But the depression of the 1930's changed our thinking. When savings were wiped out and families and individuals had to go on relief for lack of unemployment insurance, we accepted the principle of government social security. We still believe that government alone should not be called upon to provide complete social security. The inadequacies of the government system give unionists an added incentive to press for realistic security through private health, welfare, and pension plans. Collective bargaining, not government, must ultimately provide the necessary protection against the deficiencies of the economic system.

MANAGEMENT'S REVERSAL

For similar reasons, the A.F. of L. has turned to the political arena. So long as our relations with employers were wholly in the economic field, political action occupied a small role in the affairs of the A.F. of L. To be sure, we have never been nonpolitical. We have spoken before Congress and endorsed candidates for office. But until a few years ago we had no formal machinery for political action, and we made no systematic effort to educate our members on the role of government in restricting union action. The turning point was reached in 1947 when Congress adopted Taft-Hartley.

Behind this action of Congress was a change in the strategy of anti-union employers and their trade associations—the employers' unions. These employers chose the new battleground —the legislative halls—and forced the trade-union movement into the political arena. This decision by management to transfer labor-management relations from the arena of private enterprise into that of government was a reversal of the position hitherto taken by management.

For their own part, employers point to the Wagner Act of 1935 as evidence that the trade-union movement was the first to seek the protection of government. But this argument is false for two reasons. In the first place, Congress acted in 1935 in response to revelations by the La Follette Committee of the destruction of workers' civil rights by anti-union employers. The picture of industrial warfare—complete with hired armies of thugs using tear gas, propaganda, spies, and all the other paraphernalia of military campaigns—was so revolting that Congress stepped in to eliminate this evil. The Wagner Act, however, did not create any substantive rights. The right of workers to organize and choose their own representatives is inherent in our system of government. But these rights often proved to be abstract, meaningless phrases; employers could frustrate these rights through unfair exercise of their superior economic power. The definitions of unfair labor practices in the Wagner Act were not legislative imaginations. They were the sum of over fifty years of hard history. Even if the Wagner Act was, as claimed, unfair to employers—that in itself presents no sound basis for writing a law that is unfair to workers.

In the second place, the argument is false because there was no effort by the A.F. of L. to enter politics as an organized force until after the enactment of the Taft-Hartley law of 1947. The A.F. of L.'s League for Political Education was not established until 1948.

IN POLITICS TO STAY

But we shall remain in politics. The fact that we do so does not mean that the A.F. of L. will be tied to any political party. Nor does it close off any particular road in politics. I do not think the membership of the A.F. of L. is thinking now in terms of a national political party sponsored by labor. Yet if the action of the two major parties leaves us no alternative in our efforts to safeguard and raise the living standards of the workers, labor will go as far as it must down that political road.

This stand does not preclude labor's support of Republican candidates. Although the A.F. of L. endorsed the Democratic candidate for President in 1952 and has generally found itself in sympathy with more Democratic congressional candidates than Republican, it has actually supported a number of Republican candidates both for Congress and for state offices. Certainly, if one looks at American politics in historical perspective, and notes the shift in thinking of sections of the Republican party, one finds more areas of political agreement among the bulk of voters regarding major domestic programs than there were twenty-five years ago. And probably more areas of common agreement than disagreement. But differences do exist. Our sole principle has been, is, and will be to seek the election—without regard to party labels—of those who believe as we do in an economic system based on prosperity at the lower rungs of the economic ladder, and to oppose those who hold otherwise.

BETTER AMERICA, BETTER WORLD

As America looks forward to 1980 there could be no goal more worthy than demonstrating to the world moral leadership. Sharing our wealth and the methods by which we create it is but an act of humanitarianism. Proof by demonstration of our adherence to principles of morality is the test of America's sincerity as a member of the world family of nations.

For example, here at home we must speed up progress toward wiping out racialism in all its forms and colors. Man—made in the image of God—has no particular kind of color, hair, or facial structure. Until our actions—not merely our words—demonstrate that America will not tolerate racialism, we cannot adequately provide the moral leadership that the free world so sorely needs.

Of all the people on earth we in America have the greatest opportunity to make the future measure up to the highest ideals of mankind. The voluntary cooperation of labor and management in a free society can carry us far toward the attainment of this goal for all people. The obstructions in the path to cooperation are not insurmountable. There is but a minority of employers who need drop their antagonism to the right of free men to choose trade-unionism as a way of life. Then, as truly free men, labor and management may join in a constructive effort to lay down simple rules of decency and to unite in promoting mutual advances.

The American Federation of Labor stands today for the same ideals and principles that have proved so sound and constructive during all its past years. We have never lost faith in the United States of America and its Constitution dedicated to human liberty. In the light of that continuing faith, we not only expect America to lead the way for millions of people literally hungry for freedom and democracy, but we also expect that the years ahead will bring a better and even better America.

NATHAN M. PUSEY
President, Harvard University

For a Harvard president, Nathan Marsh Pusey has a somewhat unorthodox past. He was born in Council Bluffs, Iowa, went to a public high school, and was summoned to the Harvard presidency from the presidency of Lawrence College, in Appleton, Wisconsin. He is, however, a Harvard graduate, and he earned his doctorate there (in Greek history). In Cambridge, he came under the influence of the great humanist and conservative, Irving Babbitt.

Pusey, thereafter, began a service in the field of education that covers twenty-seven years, as scholar, teacher, and administrator. He presides now over one of the most distinguished, and certainly one of the most heterogeneous, faculties in the world. He is thus well qualified to speak on the tremendous problems that loom over American education and the ends toward which it should point. Dr. Pusey speaks characteristically in a mild and unimpassioned voice. Earnest, still youthful-looking at forty-eight, he has, nevertheless, impressed his quiet personality on all of his colleagues, as he is impressing his ideas on the country's oldest institution of higher learning.

The Exploding World of Education

BY NATHAN M. PUSEY

To ask anyone in the field of education to look twenty-five years ahead and consider the future goals of U.S. schools and colleges is to invite the creation of another utopia. The educator may dream and ask some idealistic questions. Will the social standing of teachers be improved by that time? Will they be paid what they are worth? Will the general public have acquired an increased respect for learning, especially humanistic learning? Will the people have become bold defenders of free inquiry?

One can hope for a day when a large number of the ablest college graduates every year will choose to become teachers. One can hope for a time when basic science will command more, not less, respect than technological application; when professional schools will turn out educated men and women with full awareness of the broadest reaches of their work; and when scientists and others will once more be able to communicate with each other around the globe, free from the restrictions that mark our troubled times. In that new day neglected studies of areas like Asia and Africa will take their proper place in the school and college program. The humanities, with their power to illuminate the spirit of man, will be held in no less esteem than the natural and behavioral sciences. More people will speak and understand the tongues of their fellow men. Informed and interested teachers and students will dispassionately but eagerly debate ethical and religious questions.

The arts will flourish in society—and perhaps people may even still read books. The educator hopes that he is not day-dreaming.

THE CLOSEMOUTHED YOUNGER GENERATION

The effects of education are released slowly, as if by a time fuse, so that the true character of a particular educational endeavor is seen only after the passage of years. The most that we can really know about the next quarter-century is that by 1980 a considerable fraction of the leadership of the country will have passed to men and women who are now coming out of the colleges and professional schools. One thought should give special pause to all educators: we shall not know fully until 1980 whether our contemporary educational effort has been good.

My personal conviction is that recent generations of college students have been at least as able and as serious in college as their predecessors. They have not said much. To some of the older generation their general behavior has seemed excessively relaxed and casual. They have not been especially eager to bestow trust in people or in principles. Certainly they have not been impressed by pretensions to virtue on the part of anyone —political leaders, writers, or even teachers. But beneath a surface manner they seem to me to run as deep as many earlier generations—and they may well be wiser. Most college graduates enter upon their adult careers resolved to work for a better world. Perhaps this generation, precisely because it is relatively unencumbered with illusions about human behavior, will be inclined to persist longer in such constructive effort. If so, it may be that by 1980 there will be a little less crassness, bombast, bigotry, and ill temper in the world, a little more disposition to be reasonable, than has sometimes been true in the past.

64

The Exploding World of Education

American education has been in a process of rapid development since its beginning. Since 1870 the most conspicuous occurrence has been the development and spread of the comprehensive high school, the aim of which, now almost realized, is to draw into its care the whole of an age group. This was a major revolution, and like all revolutions was attended by much heated discussion.

A few people, like those whose distorted ideas lead them to inveigh against the use of United Nations materials in schools, have gone so far as to see a sinister plot underlying the revolution. Others with equal vehemence now cry out that there is a conservative counterrevolution. Claims and counterclaims are made in books, articles, and speeches attacking U.S. schools and colleges from both sides.

At the bottom of much of this contentiousness can be found a failure to recognize that our American educational scheme, designed to provide for all, or most, of the members of an age group, must sometimes suffer in comparison with a program designed for a small, highly selected, and carefully prepared clientele. In most European countries today, for example, fewer than fifty out of every thousand young people go on to higher education—and these only after careful distillation by a long process of rigorous training and competitive examination. In the U.S., on the other hand, we are already approaching the time when one out of every four young Americans will go on to some kind of college. With all its shortcomings and difficulties, there are considerable advantages in our practice—especially for a democratic, technological nation.

Most of us went to a public school, quite unaware at the time that we were participating in a revolution. It is startling now, however, to note that between 1890 and 1952 the proportion of the age group attending high school rose from 3.8 per cent to 65.3 per cent, the numbers in the public high schools from less than 203,000 to nearly 7,700,000 and the number of high schools from a few thousand to almost 24,000. It is not surprising that during this time the curriculum underwent expansion and diversification, and that the old so-called "college preparatory course" was found unsuited to the enormous new spread in interests and abilities.

Now many Americans are beginning to wonder if the movement to extend the period of formal education for "all American youth" is to be pushed further to include the college experience. It is clear we have already taken substantial steps in this direction. In 1900 less than 5 per cent of those of college age went to college; their numbers were only 230,000. By 1930 there were about one million students enrolled in colleges. Today there are 2,500,000 in college and this is expected to double within the next fifteen years. It is very possible that before the end of the century one out of every two Americans will insist on "going to college." *

Meanwhile we hear frequent assertions that too many young people are enrolling in college and, indeed, there is something faddish in the way many are swept on from high school into an experience for which they are poorly prepared and have no heart. It is difficult to refute the charge that there are people in college who make too little use of their opportunity. But it is also true that there are many young people qualified for college who do not attend, and that many who begin poorly in college come alive as they go along.

---

* *The statistics on those "going to college" today include an astonishing array of institutions: four-year liberal-arts colleges, two-year junior colleges, art schools, technical institutions, schools that mix courses in general education with professional and vocational courses in a variety of proportions.*

The Exploding World of Education

Since the end of World War II, few communities have escaped the burden of building additional elementary schools and increasing their teaching staffs. Though this task is still far from completed, today the urgent need is for more high-school classrooms and teachers. Within three more years the problem will have engulfed the colleges.

Merely to maintain the present quality of college education it will probably be necessary to double the number of college teachers within the ten years from 1960 to 1970. We may have to duplicate the existing physical facilities that have been acquired slowly during three hundred years. The cost of this will be many billions of dollars (one estimate: $15 billion). It is not surprising if leaders in education seem sometimes to stand disconcerted before this prospect, or to speak with confused voices, wondering where an answer is to be found.

The difficulties will not be over by 1980, for the road to which we are committed will still be broadening before us. Not then, any more than now, shall we be able to turn back from the vastly expanded educational operation to which we are being carried not only by the pressure of increasing population (76 million in 1900; by 1980 over 200 million), but also by technological advances. These advances continue to come at an accelerating pace. The process, based on the multiplication of scientific knowledge that is shaping our world, begins in education and, in turn, feeds on and demands more education. Thus there is a certain inevitability, a kind of compulsion, governing the development of education in America. As we look at the expanding technological future we should rejoice to be going ahead; but we may be excused, too, if at times we become quizzical about the end.

Whatever their professed aims in the past, colleges have

usually been pathways to economic advance for those who attended them. It is statistically true today, for example, that the person who attends college may expect to earn upwards of $100,000 more during his lifetime than the one who does not. At present more than ever before our national life is motivated by economic calculations, and at the same time the expanding technology has contributed to making education almost unashamedly vocational. Applied science has created a technological society and, along with it, an almost insatiable demand for more and more recruits with more and more specialized, and technical, education. Industry tells us that 30,000 newly trained engineers are required each year to keep our machine society running. Obviously the vocational pressures on higher education, always formidable, will increase.

IF INDUSTRY MEANS IT

But today it should be transparently clear to all that our first need is less for specialists than for widely diffused wisdom and reliability in society. This means that specialized technical knowledge and the broad understanding and moral purpose historically associated with liberal education can no longer be kept separated. Nor can liberal education be ignored or held to be of slight importance. The demand for the professionally trained—engineers, doctors, teachers, administrators—does not slacken. But reports and demands coming into the colleges indicate that some search is being made for more people who, beyond minimum professional requirements, can be counted upon also to bring to their tasks imagination, human understanding, a sense of adventure, integrity, devotion, and an awareness of where their activity fits into larger wholes.

Thus one of our primary needs is to join liberal and professional education, or at least see to it that the latter is deeply penetrated by the former. Both kinds of education are needed

68

by society and in public life. It will not be sufficient merely to pay lip service to liberal education, or to have its praises sung by people who do not understand or fully trust it. If industry really means what it says about searching increasingly for liberally educated professionals, then it is looking for men and women who have been exposed to the lessons of industry to the insights of poetry—perhaps even to art!—and to the questions and convictions of philosophy and religion. Among them will be found those professional men and women, morally rooted, who are able to see their contributions in relation to the contributions of others, and who will have learned to acknowledge a wide range of relevancies both in their own lives and in society.

The character of our education has changed with our society. Wasting time in lamenting the passing of an earlier, more restricted, more "classical" period is of little profit. It is not likely again to be possible, nor in my judgment would it be wise, to try to cut back or restrict the numbers of those who are permitted to make what they can of the advantages of formal education, beyond high school. Education has the urgent responsibility, not yet adequately acknowledged, to provide both an opportunity for many and an exacting test for those who can run a faster race and want to go further than their fellows.

It is a truism that the continued growth in quality of civilization depends less on numbers (even numbers of engineers) than on fresh insights, extraordinary efforts, and novel achievements by a few individuals of exceptional ability who, having received the necessary exacting training, are encouraged to go beyond average attainment. Thus, although our future educational practice must make place for large numbers, it is of even greater importance that we now turn more seriously to the additional task of developing an exciting and demanding kind of formal education, designed fully to draw out the ablest members of each age group. This is the most difficult problem confronting American education in the next quarter-century. For it is the exceptional person—one might almost say the eccentric person—who all along has been opening the way toward a fuller life for all of us. We ignore him at our cost.

WANTED: GOOD TEACHERS

If the educational experiences that lead to development in individuals are to become more effective, one must begin by strengthening the quality of teaching. Devotion, knowledge, imagination, quick intelligence, patience, concern for others, awareness of beauty, grasp on principle, attractive personality —these are the great qualities that make creative teachers.

Thus a major problem confronting education is to attract more such people—to find them, prepare them, and encourage them to stick at the task.

Classrooms in which there are teachers with no exceptional gifts are places merely to keep young people, not to educate them. The absence of vitalizing personal qualities in the education process is more deeply and tragically injurious than a thoughtless adult world has yet been ready to recognize. Injury is done in terms of stunted, frustrated, and twisted personal lives. But there is also social injury. When a student's imagination is not stirred, or when he merely suffers through schools, he not only fails to develop whatever potential may be in him, he is actually being prepared to join those who are indifferent or hostile to the claims of intellect. Their numbers, always too large, impose a heavy drag on every effort to advance.

ALMOST FORGOTTEN PROFESSION

We have not yet been sufficiently aroused to do much about the waste that goes on in our classrooms. Nor shall we effect improvement so long as society continues to place such relatively slight value, measured in salary and prestige, on the services of teachers. During the past twenty-five years the salaries of teachers in colleges, measured in terms of stable purchasing power, rose about one-sixth as much as the rise of per capita income measured in the same way. Parents today complain of the current "high" cost of higher education; yet the rise in per capita income in this country in recent decades has been roughly three times as great as the rise in college tuition. The effect of this disparity on the teaching profession is all too apparent.

There are 70,000 school districts in the U.S., and approximately 1,800 institutions of higher education. Virtually all of them are having difficulty in finding enough teachers. Many communities are beginning to take steps to improve the standing and economic condition of teachers. These efforts must be multiplied and accelerated. Efforts already made in a number of colleges to interest more young people in the teaching profession must be intensified. From the demonstrated readiness of able young people to respond when the teaching career is fairly described to them, there is reason to hope that—bad as the situation has looked and still looks—the number of good teachers can and will be considerably increased.

And more effective and imaginative ways must be found to prepare them to teach. It is not a superabundance of technical courses that makes a good teacher. The chief requirement is a bright and energetic individual who continues to be deeply affected by educational experience.

WHERE'S THE MONEY?

Finding more adequate ways to finance education is not the least troublesome of the problems. Whether or not the sums are enough, the cities and states are spending enormous amounts on education. Large federal funds also find their way into education and will continue to do so, for there are many things the government needs that can be acquired only from educational institutions. At the same time there are very few public institutions that could operate without some private funds, from alumni, foundations, and industry. It is probable that the phenomenon of "mixed" support will continue to grow.

In this period of gathering difficulty there has come a growing and refreshing recognition by the business world of its dependence upon education. Increasingly, large corporations have been building their own technical and specialized educational programs. This is all to the good. But the need for the more basic and general kind of education that only the colleges and universities can supply is not lessened by these efforts. It is indeed encouraging to find business corporations beginning now to contribute more responsibly to the colleges' support.

WITH NO STRINGS ATTACHED

Industry's early efforts along this line tended to be directed to technical and professional institutions, not infrequently in the form of grants to support research. These are important and fortunately they continue. But now there is more recognition that the chief product of the colleges and universities is selected, educated men and women, and that in the preparation of these people the contribution of the undergraduate liberal-arts college is no less important that that of the graduate and professional school—indeed, may even have a prior kind of importance. Hence business and industrial corporations are now becoming interested in general college scholarship programs. The most perceptive of the corporations also include contributions toward the basic expenses of the educational institutions, for there are very few colleges and universities that do not have to make a significant contribution to the cost of the education of each of their students. A further movement toward unrestricted contributions has brought a new heart to trustees and administrative officials. These are grants for the general expenses of an institution, which leave it to the institution itself to decide how the funds should be used.

The number of plans already adopted by business and industrial corporations to help the colleges has increased sharply in recent years. Additional programs are in process of formulation. Conspicuous examples are the national scholarship program of General Motors, the effort of General Electric to encourage alumni giving by employees, systems of outright grants to selected institutions by Standard Oil of New Jersey, Westinghouse, and U.S. Steel, and a new fellowship program set up by Procter & Gamble. These are only a few among many. Crucial assistance has been given to higher education by the large private philanthropic foundations. An outstanding example of the latter kind of support is the allocation of large sums by the Ford Foundation to be given to a selected list of colleges and universities on a matching basis to help improve teachers' salaries.

NOT DEAD YET

Such encouragement comes most happily perhaps for private and independent institutions. Many have been wondering how these institutions are to survive. As the pressure of numbers must almost inevitably work toward uniformity, and toward providing for the more obvious needs of society, we shall, I hope, find ourselves placing greater value on the strong independent institutions, which can work intensively and carefully with small numbers. The number of American students at the college level or above has long been almost equally divided between those in publicly and privately supported institutions of higher learning, although at the secondary-school level the proportion attending the privately supported is very small indeed. The trend has been away from the private to the public institutions and will undoubtedly have gone further in this direction by 1980. In consequence, the private institutions will have an even greater responsibility for maintaining the qualitative level of education.

People who have attended privately controlled institutions are becoming increasingly aware of their responsibility to make it possible for later generations to enjoy what they enjoyed. The amount of alumni donations to private educational institutions has shown a steady annual increase for a long time, and it is now reaching very significant proportions.

Thus it is possible to affirm that in a confused situation, where everything seems at first glance to be at the mercy of numbers and public impulse, there are forces working along more discriminating lines, along lines essential to the well-being of the whole. The private, independent way of life is far from dead in the U.S., and lamentation over private colleges and universities at this time would be definitely premature.

Education has had a considerable hand in creating our technological society. But precisely because of its successes in this direction education has come to take on too shallow a meaning for many of us. Because of the enormous material benefits that have accrued to the nation through education, the view is widely held that the production of specific benefits is the true business of education. There is also a simple faith that somehow the discoveries that lead on to advances

74

in economic and social life, and promise new goods for the future, will continue to spring of themselves from laboratories and test tubes, or can be had by the mere expenditure of money. Neither view is true.

MORE THAN MEETS THE EYE

The important consideration is always the individual human mind. It is neither technology nor the vast organization of research that will produce the desired results; at the level of application, perhaps yes, but not at the source where the fresh idea is born. Fresh ideas have always sprung from the minds of individual, unregimented men or women who are motivated by curiosity, who are properly prepared, who are in love with learning for learning's sake. This consideration by itself would justify a more discriminating concern for education on the part of Americans. But it must be more widely recognized that in the end the controlling aim of education lies beyond the service of material culture.

The age-old conflict within education about its ultimate purpose will, I fear, still be unresolved in 1980. Almost from the beginning there have been those who have believed that everything needful is said when it is stated that education's function is to serve society. They can with reason argue that education contributes to health; provides the necessary skills for making a living; imparts knowledge of a community; or, at the widest reach, teaches good citizenship. Opposed to them are the humanists who, while not explicitly denying any of these aims, resolutely insist that education needs no such justification, that it is an experience valid for its own sake, and that its proper function is simply to help individuals to grow as individuals. It has never been the intention of the latter group to imply that an individual is a lost soul if he has learned from his educational experience how to do something "useful." Education cannot escape a responsibility to pass on the knowledge and skills necessary to keep a culture alive, and to prepare individuals for activity within our social and economic life. Yet are these the final ends?

There is much more to both arguments than readily meets the eye—perhaps even different views as to what a human being is. Despite the vehemence of the partisans, the record indicates that education has always had to do both things.

The values of words are constantly shifting. A word to which extraordinarily high value is attached at the moment is "competence." On all sides we hear that what is wanted from the educational process are competent people. He would be a rash man indeed who in the face of such universal acclaim of competence would set out to make a case for incompetence, but it may be admissible to suggest that the notion of competence by itself does not exhaust the meaning to be found in the phrase "an educated man." Understanding and competence are not quite the same thing; and one can perhaps be competent without being wise.

PEOPLE, NOT SUBJECTS

The aims of education should not be exclusively, or even predominantly, defined by the needs of the economic structuring of our society. Knowledge and planning in the light of knowledge, the setting of goals on the basis of a wide range of evidence, and the working toward these goals—certainly, capacities of this kind are indispensable, and education must do what it can to develop them. But there is also a higher obligation for education to produce dedicated scholars and investigators able to advance knowledge in every field of human endeavor. Though the numbers who can aspire to this level of effort will be limited, those with the capacity to do original, basic investigation must be found, given every opportunity for their own intellectual development, and encouraged to stay at basic research in the universities in an environment of freedom and high purpose.

But even at this point the responsibility of education is not fully discharged. Its ultimate and more difficult responsibility is to ensure that learning itself, a sense of loyalty, sensitivity to beauty, broad interest, humility, patience—that these and perhaps other ancient virtues not necessarily included within competence have their very basic place, in the world and in individual lives. Though it is not easy to say how this can be done, we have learned enough to be reasonably sure it will not be done by further reducing the attention paid to humanistic studies. Since it is people, not subjects, that are of first importance in education, we are not likely to advance if the influence on education of those who care deeply for the extraordinary reaches of the human spirit is permitted to grow less.

Only teachers who have themselves become awakened to such values will know how to make this kind of learning operative in the lives of succeeding generations of young people. It is still true that in a sense this learning must "rub off" teachers, or be caught from them. And beyond all this there is the knowledge and awareness that lead to religious living. This, too, is caught, not won by effort. It is very difficult to talk about, especially among the unpersuaded. Furthermore, it is still uncertain what formal education can do to help one toward a religious life. Yet despite many difficulties, there is a growing recognition that an education that ignores this large, central, perennial, and life-giving area of human experience is a kind of play education, and finally a shallow thing. Happily, there are beginning to be signs that schools, colleges, and universities will do better in this regard in the next quarter-century than in the past.

SERVANT AND CRITIC

In the end, then, we return again to the liberally educated teacher, who is, of course, a competent professional, but who must also be something more—a person of exceptional quality. The teacher's special job is to nurture in young people the desire to extend themselves, and to help them, with their minds and wills, to grow beyond competence into full humanity. Society has cared less for such teachers than it might, and has done too little to find their successors. It is to be hoped that by 1980 there will be, in all colleges and schools, more of those men and women whose lives and values will creatively touch our children's lives, and our own.

Education is society's servant but also her tireless critic, for no civilization is ever worthy of worship. Values of crucial importance for human beings are always getting lost, or getting obscured and undervalued, in the workaday world. A complete education has a responsibility to do more than "serve society." It has to save us from ourselves.

EARL WARREN

Chief Justice of the United States

Earl Warren is the fourteenth Chief Justice of the United States. Of Scandinavian descent, he was born in Los Angeles, March 19, 1891, was educated at the University of California and its law school, practiced law in San Francisco and Oakland, became a successful prosecuting attorney, was elected state attorney general in 1938 and governor of California in 1942. He held the governorship for a record ten years and nine months, until his appointment to the Supreme Court by President Eisenhower. During his governorship, California's population nearly doubled. The popularity of his administration (he was the only man ever elected to three terms, once by nomination of both major parties) made him a national figure in the Republican party and its vice-presidential nominee in 1948. Calm, practical, hearty, persuasive, and stubborn, he has introduced a marked degree of good will and cooperation to the Court during his two years as its Chief. The most far-reaching of his Court's decisions, that in the school segregation cases, was unanimous.

The Law and the Future

BY EARL WARREN

When a man of law tries to peer through the next twenty-five years, he is struck by the probability that all legal systems, and indeed the very concept of law, will be as severely tested as ever in history. The test comes from two sides.

First, the accelerating rate of scientific and technological change in the world makes the pace of legal change look like a tortoise racing a hare. In other chapters, it has been predicted by men of science that worldwide transportation may soon become almost as rapid as communication is now; that nuclear developments can make energy almost as cheap as air; that climate control will enable us to turn the Arctic into a tropical garden or alternatively to bring on another Ice Age, as we please. These and like marvels, if achieved, will obviously revolutionize those relationships between man and man, and between man and government, which are the subject matter of the law.

The other test of law comes from the world political situation. The struggle between Communism and freedom, whether hot, cold, or lukewarm, extends not only along the physical frontiers of our civilization, but into its mind and soul, inevitably straining the fabric of all our institutions, the law included. Our legal system is woven around the freedom and dignity of the individual. A Communist state ignores these values. Ours is the difficult task of defending and strengthening these values while also pursuing a goal that sometimes appears to be in conflict with them—namely, the physical security of our nation.

Such are two formidable challenges to the law which seem to line the corridor of the next twenty-five years.

WHY THE CHALLENGES MUST BE MET

Yet no man who understands the nature and purpose of law will let these challenges go by default. There are at least three reasons why an American jurist must work, hope, and pray that the observance of law, the prestige of law, and the knowledge of law will be far more widespread a generation hence than they are now. I shall give these reasons and then proceed to suggest, as specifically as possible, how I think that hope can be fulfilled.

First of all, the U.S., as Americans have always known and loved it, cannot subsist without law. Our Constitution was designed chiefly by lawyers; it was given bone and sinew by great jurists like John Marshall; and we owe the continuity of our social existence to the respect for law of which our reverence for the Constitution is the symbol and sign. Cicero defined a commonwealth as "an agreement of law and a community of interest." Without their agreement of law, Americans might still have some community of interest, but it would unquestionably take one of those barbaric forms in which order is kept by force alone, and in which the freedom of the individual and the consent of the governed are ignored.

In the second place, it is not just the U.S. that needs law, it is the entire world. The world's chief need in these next decades will be peace and order; and of all human institutions, law has the best historical claim to satisfy this need. Isaiah said that peace is the work of justice. It was an English axiom, framed by Coke, that certainty is the mother of quiet. Justice and certainty are twin aims of the law. When the U.S. entered the late World War, British soldiers sent the following message to our soldiers: "We welcome you as brothers in the struggle to make sure that the world shall be ruled by the force of law, and not by the law of force." Until the millennium, when all men shall be ruled by Christian love, no other means of social peace but these two—the law of force or the force of law—are likely to be known to man.

The third reason the great mid-century challenges to the law must be met is simply this: the nature of man. In all times and places he has had a sense of justice and a desire for justice. Any child expresses this fact of nature with his first judgment that this or that "isn't fair." A legal system is simply a mature and sophisticated attempt, never perfected but always capable of improvement, to institutionalize this sense of justice and to free men from the terror and unpredictability of arbitrary force. Unfortunately, the same human nature that craves justice and freedom under law is too often willing to deny them to others. Thus the struggle for law is never-ending, and our generation is inevitably engaged in it.

The Supreme Court building in Washington is adorned with many statues and friezes. Among the figures represented are Menes, Hammurabi, Moses, Solomon, Lycurgus, Solon, Draco, Confucius, and Octavian, all lawgivers to people who needed and wanted law before the time of Christ; also Justinian, Mohammed, Charlemagne, King John, St. Louis, Grotius, Blackstone, Napoleon, and Marshall, lawgivers since the time of Christ. The history of law is as old as human nature. By the same token, its proper scope is the world. In fact there is no tribe on the face of the earth, however primitive, and no nation, however tyrannical, that is without some customary or formal code of crime and punishment. The problem of law in the next twenty-five years, therefore, is not so much to introduce law anywhere as it is to improve, strengthen, and civilize law everywhere. Especially must we broaden the scope of that youngest and most fragile of great legal systems, the law of nations.

What is the American share of this great task? To understand that, we must first understand our own legal system, its strengths and weaknesses.

THE INHERITANCE WE BUILD ON

We Americans are peculiarly fortunate in our legal inheritance. One ancestor of our system is Roman law, of which the legal historian Maine said that it had "the longest known history of any set of human institutions," during which history it was "progressively modified for the better." The nearer ancestor of our system is English law, which has for centuries kept peace throughout an empire and commonwealth wider and more complex than the Roman. Our American modification of these systems has served us equally well. With all its imperfections, it can be called an outstanding success. Of the many characteristics of our legal system that can be given credit for this success, three seem to me especially significant.

First, our legal system has been an organic growth, and not the overnight creation of any individual genius. The Founding Fathers wrote our Constitution in a single summer, but in doing so they borrowed unashamedly from long-dead lawmakers and political philosophers from Moses and Aristotle to Locke and Montesquieu. In fact they created no novel or untested principles, but chose the best of those already known; and that is one reason their work has endured. The idea of due process, for example, they owed to Magna Charta; the idea of habeas corpus came to them from sources lost in the mists of the Middle Ages. The natural rights of man explicitly asserted by our Founding Fathers had long been the common-law rights of Englishmen.

Moreover, having written our Constitution, the Founding

Fathers did not use it to abolish and replace the laws to which Americans had been accustomed. The new national system was organically grafted on to the state legal systems, not only those of English, but also those of Latin origin, and has grown along with them to this day. I have already mentioned some of the alien lawgivers whose figures appropriately adorn our Supreme Court building, and others could be mentioned —Capito and Labeo, Sabinus and Proclus, Gaius and Ulpian —whose very names are known only to scholars of the law, but who made their contributions to its coral-like growth. And the gallery of American law is not complete without representatives of our own colonial, frontier, and state legal experience: eloquent lawyers like Andrew Hamilton, who defended John Peter Zenger and the freedom of the press; brave judges like William Cushing, who advanced alone against the bayonets of Shays' Rebellion and opened the Massachusetts Court; clear thinkers like Chancellor Kent, whose opinions were carried by the authority of reason far beyond the borders of New York. An organic system like ours requires the faithful work of many men, both famous and unknown.

A second reason for the success of our legal system is its adaptability to changing circumstance. As Pollock said, all courts have a duty, which ours generally try to perform, "to keep the rules of law in harmony with the enlightened common sense of the nation." Even the bicycle forced new definitions of negligence in civil suits; and the thousands of other changes forced by later technological developments indicate that our law can keep up with the still greater changes ahead —so long as "the common sense of the nation" can be discerned. Our judges are not monks or scientists, but participants in the living stream of our national life, steering the law between the dangers of rigidity on the one hand and of formlessness on the other. Legal scholars may still debate whether the life of the law is reason, as Coke maintained, or experience, as Holmes claimed. I think it is both. Our system faces no theoretical dilemma but a single continuous problem: how to apply to ever changing conditions the never changing principles of freedom.

So far as the Constitution is concerned, it has demonstrated again and again its capacity for adaptation to the most challenging new conditions. Under John Marshall's leadership, it proved it could mold a strong national government, at a time when such a government was needed to protect American liberties. Later the Constitution had to find a path for those same liberties through the iron mazes of our industrial revolution. And while this quest continues through new electronic mazes, still another challenge confronts the Constitution: must a nation that is now the strongest in the world demand, for its own further strength and security, a sacrifice by its own citizens of their ancient liberties? This problem haunts the work of all our courts these days. But the Constitution exists for the individual as well as for the nation. I believe it will prove itself adaptable to this new challenge.

There is a third reason for the success of our legal system: while adaptable to our changing national needs, it serves a greater and unchanging cause. That cause is human justice. Ever since Hammurabi published his code to "hold back the strong from oppressing the weak," the success of any legal system is measured by its fidelity to the universal ideal of justice. Theorists beset us with other definitions of law: that it is a mask of privilege, or the judge's private prejudice, or the will of the stronger. But the ideal of justice survives all such myopic views, for as Cicero said, "we are born to it."

The American legal system was nurtured in this ideal of justice and could not last without it. We have in fact accepted not only the rule of law but, through our unique practice of judicial review of legislation, the reign of law. We have done so in the full knowledge that judges are fallible, procedures slow, and the Constitution itself a product of compromise; but in the faith that it is better to make our final decisions in the name of an eternal ideal. Our courts have occasionally misused their great power of review, but never to the point of justifying its forfeiture. They are kept in line with the other branches of government not only by the words of the Constitution, but by a tradition of self-restraint and impersonality.

LAW AND THE GREAT TRADITION

The American constitutional system is in the great tradition which places the fundamental law above the will of the government. This tradition began with the dawn of our civilization. The people of Israel governed themselves as a federation of tribes, without any central government, under a Constitution—the Covenant they had made with Jehovah. Even after they chose a king ("that we also may be like all the nations") they kept the tradition because the king, too, lived and ruled under the Covenant. When Rome was young, many a similar commonwealth and republic flourished around the Mediterranean; but Rome survived them all because it employed and extended the rule of law, thus making its greatest contribution to our civilization. When the Renaissance broke the mold of medieval Europe, England was not the only monarchy that gave promise of constitutional development. But England alone avoided a serious relapse into despotism, because England secured its public order and individual freedom under the law.

The sign of this great tradition, the tradition which places the fundamental law above the will of the government, is an independent judiciary. We associate it with our system of separated powers and judicial review; but other nations have maintained the tradition with other forms of government. Britain's system of parliamentary supremacy, for example, can override but does not overawe British justice.

Why, then, have some nations maintained and strengthened the great tradition and not others? For one reason only, that the people were determined to remain free and to keep the law above the government. When the Hitler occupation tried to bend the Supreme Court of Norway to its will, the entire Court risked death by resigning. This act, I am sure, did as much to preserve independent justice for Norway as did *Marbury* vs. *Madison* for the U.S., or as Coke's defiance of his dictatorial King did for England. No form of government, however nearly perfect, can itself secure justice and freedom under law for any country. The true safeguard is the spirit and devotion of the people, a passion for justice and freedom that is widely shared and deeply felt.

To summarize: Americans have one of the great legal systems, but not a monopoly of the sense of justice, which is universal; nor have we a permanent copyright on the means of securing justice, for it is the spirit and not the form of law that keeps justice alive. But as a nation directly challenged by the march of a revolutionary technology, and also by a reactionary antagonist representing the law of force, we have a vital interest in defending and extending the rule of law throughout the world. How then can we go about it?

NEEDED REFORMS OF OUR SYSTEM

Two generations ago Dean Ames of the Harvard Law School pointed out that "the spirit of reform which during the last six hundred years has been bringing our system of law more and more into harmony with moral principles has not yet achieved its perfect work"; and he urged that past advances should encourage effort for future improvement. This advice still needs to be heeded. The proud inscription on our federal courts—Equal Justice Under Law—remains our goal but is not fully secured to all our citizens. The rights promised them by our Constitution are not yet perfected. Some of the defects in our system are inherited; others keep creeping in. Justice, like freedom, needs constant vigilance.

Justice delayed is often justice denied. This kind of denial is a growing problem in our federal courts. Some calendars are so crowded that litigants cannot be sure of trial within four years or more. To our Judicial Conference (composed of the Chief Justice and the Chief Judges of the circuit courts) this has been a problem of increasing concern. It will require a combined effort by the bench, the bar, and the litigating public, as well as some help from Congress, to clear this growing backlog and keep the channels of justice open.

Unequal justice is a contradiction in terms. Yet access to justice is unequal in parts of our country. Suspects are sometimes arrested, tried, and convicted without being adequately informed of their right to counsel. Even when he knows of this right, many a citizen cannot afford to exercise it. There are barely half enough public defenders, legal-aid societies, or other methods available to perfect this right.

American law is pockmarked with other procedural flaws and anachronisms. We have recently made some progress in simplifying methods of appeal in the federal courts, but much remains to be done. Thanks to outside underwriting, our entire system of administering criminal justice is undergoing a detailed survey by the American Bar foundation. The facts already known warrant a continuing crusade by the legal profession for fairer and speedier procedures.

Lawyers are officers of the court and therefore servants of

justice. Now that the more cynical forms of "legal realism" are growing less fashionable, it is to be hoped that fewer lawyers will regard their professional training as a mere means of livelihood. But cynicism and apathy are not confined to our profession. Since the instinct of justice is universal, every citizen, lawyer or not, can serve justice by living more consciously in its spirit, and by keeping his own vigilant watch on the rights he shares with his fellow citizen. Solon, asked how justice could be secured in Athens, replied, "If those who are not injured feel as indignant as those who are."

WHOSE BILL OF RIGHTS?

This is especially good advice at a time when our Bill of Rights is under subtle and pervasive attack, as at present. The attack comes not only from without, but from our own indifference and failure of imagination. Minorities whose rights are threatened are quicker to band together in their own defense than in the defense of other minorities. The same is true, with less reason, of segments of the majority. Churchmen are quick to defend religious freedom; lawyers were never so universally aroused as by President Roosevelt's Court bill; newspapers are most alert to civil liberties when there is a hint of press censorship in the air. And educators become perturbed at every attempt to curb academic freedom. But too seldom do all of these become militant when ostensibly the rights of only one group are threatened. They do not always react to the truism that when the rights of any individual or group are chipped away, the freedom of all erodes.

The moral is that if each minority, each professional group, and each citizen would imagine himself in the other's shoes, everybody's rights would have firmer support. The beginning of justice is the capacity to generalize and make objective one's private sense of wrong, thus turning it to public account. The pursuit of justice is not the vain pursuit of a remote abstraction; it is a continuing direction for our daily conduct.

Thus it is that when the generation of 1980 receives from us the Bill of Rights, the document will not have exactly the same meaning it had when we received it from our fathers. We will pass on a better Bill of Rights or a worse one, tarnished by neglect or burnished by growing use. If these rights are real, they need constant and imaginative application to new situations. For example: the security procedures set up to protect the federal government have been extended to the point where more than eight million Americans * must undergo them. As the system expands, everyone is more closely affected by the balance we strike between security and freedom. Injustices carry a wider import. The Bill of Rights must be measured daily against this new problem.

NO U.S. MONOPOLY

By thus improving the administration of justice and strengthening liberty under law in our own country, we will make our greatest single contribution to the promotion of law elsewhere in the world. For as long as the U.S. leads the forces of freedom in the world's great ideological struggle, our institutions will remain under a global spotlight, and what we do will speak much louder than what we say. If our actions continuously testify to our belief in justice, other free nations will be fortified in their pursuit of the same ideal.

A vital concern for the ideal of justice is what all legal

---

* *Including some three million members of the armed forces; 2,400,000 civilian employees of the U.S. Government; and nearly three million employees of defense contractors. If the families of these people are included, the number of Americans now subject to federal security investigation might be as high as 20 million.*—EDITORS.

91

systems most need today. The variety of legal systems need not trouble us; they are like different languages. Some languages are subtler or richer, some more logical or straightforward than others; but all serve the common purpose of communication. So all good legal systems, with their varying histories and environments, serve justice as their people see it; and the best of them serve the great tradition of government under law. But as languages can enrich and extend communication by translations and borrowings, so too can legal systems. The promotion of law in the world will therefore benefit from a revival of comparative jurisprudence, a revival in which American lawyers are already taking an active part.

Twice in our history, in 1883 and 1915, the Lord Chief Justice of England has sat by invitation as an observer on the bench of the U.S. Supreme Court. I was accorded a similar courtesy in Norway, where I heard proceedings before their Supreme Court; and I also met with the members of Germany's constitutional court in their conference room. At Salzburg, I visited the seminar where American institutions, including American law, are interpreted to deeply interested students from all parts of free Europe; Chief Judge Magruder of our First Circuit Court of Appeals was a recent lecturer. Leading law schools both here and in Europe are giving increased attention to comparative law.

It seems clear that this mutual interest and curiosity can profitably be carried much further. Moslem lands, for example, have old and well-developed legal systems about which American jurists know very little, as do Moslems about ours. An agreement among different cultures to exchange full information on basic points of comparative law—such as why, and under what conditions, a man may be jailed—should lead to considerable self-examination and improvement on all sides. In investigating why a thief may have his hand cut off in Saudi Arabia, or be branded on the forehead in other countries, we might also be led to study some debatable forms of punishment still used in some of our states. Habeas corpus, a right we regard as fundamental to a free society, is not so regarded in some other democracies; why not? Why are British court procedures so much more orderly and rapid than ours? To pursue such inquiries in a spirit of mutual truth-seeking could surely yield good results. All of us have much to teach and much to learn.

WORLD LAW AND THE U.N.

The United Nations exists because civilized nations prefer orderly, rational, and peaceful procedures in the settlement of disputes. This preference is the cradle of law. The U.N. can become the growing point of a true international legal system, but only as it grows around the ideal of justice. The U.N. must therefore bend its efforts to make justice the keystone of its arch.

Three ways to do this suggest themselves. First, as justice is a universal goal, so should the membership of the U.N. transcend its origin as a league of wartime allies, and become as nearly universal as an acceptance of the charter obligations permits. Second, peaceful procedures imply that agreements will be inviolable. There will be great need for the strict honoring of U.N. agreements in the next twenty-five years, and the nations with the best record in this respect will have done the most to advance the cause of justice under law. Third, more and more international questions can become justiciable, giving a steadily wider jurisdiction to the World Court.

The U.N. has inevitably been an arena of power politics and ideological struggle. This need not discourage those who hope to see it develop into a focus of world law. It was during one of history's earlier great struggles, the Thirty Years War, that Hugo Grotius of Holland brought to birth those concepts of international law that were to moderate international behavior for three centuries. The U.N. has not succeeded in writing a generally satisfactory Bill of Human Rights. This does not mean that there is no measure of international agreement on this vital subject. Recently an International Congress of Jurists, composed of lawyers, judges, and teachers from forty-nine nations, showed an astonishing unanimity in their so-called Act of Athens, defining the basic characteristics of a free system. They declared that the state is subject to the law, and owes its citizens the means to enforce their rights; that judges should uphold the rule of law in entire political independence; that lawyers of the world should insist on a fair trial for every accused; and that the rights of the individual, to be protected by the rule of law, include freedom of speech, press, worship, assembly, association, and free elections. If by 1980 this writ should run through all the nations whose lawyers helped frame it, then indeed will the great tradition of government under law be established beyond challenge in our world.

Whether or not law can tame the ideological struggles of this era, there is another broad field of human intercourse which can and should be brought wholly within orderly procedures. This is the economic field, where rivalries have sometimes bred wars in the past but need not again. Governments have spent millions of man-hours, as well as billions of dollars, on world economic problems since World War II. They have not solved these problems, but they are learning to manage them. New types of treaties and commissions have proliferated throughout the field of international trade, investment, and finance. Within the free world, if we have the will, these orderly procedures and expert institutions can be made to temper all economic controversies and prevent them from becoming inflammatory. We can reasonably resolve that this whole field will be subordinated to peaceful procedures during the next twenty-five years. Justice in the economic sphere often consists in finding a genuine mutuality of interest. Among the free nations, that mutuality is already great, and can be made permanent.

THE HERITAGE AND THE STRUGGLE

Such are the chief growing points from which the law may extend its influence over the affairs of men in the next generation. In doing so it faces the challenges (already mentioned) of an accelerating technology and a world political struggle for survival.

The challenge of technology to the law is largely to its rate of change. To meet it, the law need not itself get more technically complex than it is now; rather the opposite may be its best course. For in self-defense against a technology which only a few can hope to master, the average man and the common sense of justice will seek an ally in laws which all can understand. As in Blackstone's time, some knowledge of law may become "an essential part of a liberal education"; and lawyers, reaffirming their purpose in life to serve justice, may come in closer touch with the deepest springs of our democracy.

The world political struggle is more dangerous to the future of law. It is a struggle of greater proportions than Americans have known before. In some of our wars, we have briefly succumbed to the temptation of imitating the vices of our antagonist; but the national sense of justice and respect for law always returned with peace. In the present struggle between our world and Communism, the temptation to imitate totalitarian security methods is a subtle temptation that must be resisted day by day, for it will be with us as long as totalitarianism itself. The whole question of man's relation to his nation, his government, his fellow man is raised in acute and chronic form. Each of the 462 words of our Bill of Rights, the most precious part of our legal heritage, will be tested and retested.

By 1980 that heritage can be stronger and brighter than ever, and the ideal of liberty and justice under law made more real in its various forms throughout the world. But it will require a new dedication and a continuing faith from all who cherish the heritage and the goal.

CRAWFORD H. GREENEWALT

President, E. I. du Pont de Nemours & Co.

Crawford Hallock Greenewalt, the polished and articulate president of du Pont, is in a position to view the coming quarter-century as both scientist and businessman. A trained chemist (M.I.T. '22), he can contemplate the technological horizon with a scientist's reasoned optimism. As chief executive of a huge (1954 sales: $1.68 billion), complex industrial corporation, however, he is less sanguine. He believes that "management is at the root of company success" and that steeply progressive personal income taxes are eroding management incentives.

The Slow, Steady Way of Progress

BY CRAWFORD H. GREENEWALT

I dislike making specific prophecies. This is not because I worry particularly about being "caught out," for in 1980 I shall be seventy-seven, with a sufficiently Olympian point of view not to care too much about the accuracy or inaccuracy of predictions made by a rash youth in his early fifties. The difficulty with specific predictions is somewhat more fundamental. In the first place they are much more likely to be wrong than right. Second, they are almost always more pessimistic than the actuality. And, finally, spectacular new developments in technology by themselves are unlikely to determine the material progress we will make over the next twenty-five years.

The errors of past prophets have been largely due, I think, to the fact that they reasoned from the framework of social and technical progress in their particular day, and they did not, and in fact could not, take into account the new technologies that were just over their horizon. Thomas Jefferson, for example, in announcing the Louisiana Purchase, felt that the territory might be fully occupied after twenty-five generations—i.e., along about 2600 A.D. He could not have foreseen that the invention of the railroad and the steamboat would open it up to settlement within a few decades. Sir William Crookes, a very distinguished scientist, in 1898 foretold starvation for the human race through diminishing supplies of nitrogen. As things stood in his day, that was perhaps a perfectly valid prediction; but what he did not foresee was that chemistry, through the fixation of nitrogen from the air, would within a generation or so remove the threat of starvation far into the future. One of Jules Verne's prophecies did indeed come true—we do have submarines—but, on the other hand, it now seems pretty silly to think of taking eighty days to go around the world, and the thought of visiting the moon by traveling in a projectile shot out of a conventional gun seems positively childish when viewed against today's realities.

THE GROWTH RATIO

Fortunately we do not have to visualize the precise shape of things to come to be able to predict with confidence another twenty-five years or more of growth and prosperity. The past supplies us with indicators that, though not particularly exciting, are sound and reliable. This is because research and its enormous leverage in producing material benefits is the major factor that has dictated past progress and that provides the only valid basis for future growth. The chemical industry, by way of example, has been research-minded from its beginnings and has had a rate of growth substantially greater than that of industry generally. In my view this is a simple statement of cause and effect.

For the du Pont Co., I can be somewhat more quantitative. We have reasonably good figures for research expenditures year by year since 1921 and also for construction expenditures during the same period. The ratio of the two has averaged about one to three, which means that for every dollar we have spent in our laboratories we have sooner or later spent $3 for new plants, products, and processes. This ratio, incidentally, has been reasonably constant over a period during which our annual research expenditures have increased from $1 million to something over $60 million. Or if one wishes to take an over-all look, we spent in the past twenty-five years approximately $475 million on research, excluding the cost of buildings and equipment. Over the same period, expenditures for new plant and equipment have been approximately $1.4 billion. The ratio of one to three, valid both for the short and long term, can I think be extrapolated into the future with some confidence.

We like, of course, to think about research in terms of the startling new product that springs from the test tube to the accompaniment of lyric headlines. At du Pont we like to talk about moistureproof cellophane, about neoprene, and about nylon. In addition to being fodder for good publicity, these developments have certainly contributed largely to our corporate prosperity. In retrospect, however, I doubt that such individually spectacular accomplishments would account for as much as half of our growth over the last twenty-five to thirty years.

It is easy to overemphasize the new and in so doing to pay insufficient tribute to what might be called "bit-by-bit" research. By this I mean the day-to-day effort that produces results which over a short period seem inconsequential, but which over the long run are extraordinarily important. It would be my guess that the average research man in the du Pont Co. would have to work for two or three lifetimes before being associated with a development that hit the headlines. He pays his way not by the spectacular but by the bit-by-bit process of incremental accomplishment.

To be more specific, let me mention the progress of cellophane. We enjoyed headlining the invention of the moisture-proofing process that for the first time put cellophane on its commercial feet. That was a spectacular and quite extraordinary development. On the other hand, during the last twenty-five years the output of a cellophane-casting machine has been increased sixfold, the output per man-hour fifteenfold, and the pounds produced per dollar of investment have been increased sevenfold. And it is these results that have made cellophane the important product it has become today, that have put its price at a sufficiently low level to make it generally useful. During any given year, process and product improvements, while solid and sure, are likely to be completely unspectacular. Over the long term, however, they make the difference between a static and a burgeoning economy.

In summary, I hope I have been convincing in arguing that the economy of the nation is only moderately aided by the new and spectacular. Its growth on the other hand is enormously dependent upon the summation of small, sure improvements brought by unswerving devotion to research. This is the slow, steady way of progress.

As to the future, I have no doubt that research will be quite as fruitful as it has been in the past. Research is not, of course, a cash-and-carry activity in which a given expenditure can guarantee a given result, and productivity per unit of outlay may decrease as problems and the apparatus for solving them become more complex. The offset, however, lies in the growing appreciation by many industries of what technical effort can do. However one chooses to make the measurement—whether by manpower or by dollars—research has grown at a startling rate. There is now scarcely an industry without full awareness of research and its promise. Twenty years ago the chemical industry employed some 6,500 people in research work in its laboratories. There are approximately 35,000 today. The demand of all industry for competent research personnel has increased to the point where our colleges and universities are having grave difficulty in turning out qualified people in sufficient numbers. And this despite a great increase in effectiveness of the average research scientist. For in 1938 there was roughly one laboratory assistant or technician supporting six professional scientists. Today the ratio is about one to one, which means that the scientist is to that degree more free to pursue his trade—and to that degree more useful.

In research, then, lie the seeds of greatness, and the question for the next quarter-century is not whether they will germinate—for they surely will—but rather the specific directions that growth will take.

A FEW CENTS WORTH OF CHEMICALS

Specific discussion of the future of the chemical industry is made difficult by its ubiquitous nature. By and large our products do not reach the consumer directly—to be felt, seen, and admired. We supply raw materials for other industries, which they, in turn, convert, sometimes in one step, sometimes in many, to the article that the consumer at retail finally sees, wants, and uses. There is, moreover, scarcely a product (offhand I can think of none) that reaches the consumer without the chemical industry's having played some part in its production. Sometimes the touch of chemistry is light and incidental; sometimes it is heavy and obvious. Chemistry's role in the production of such things as nylon, plastics, or synthetic rubber has been so well publicized that it has become somewhat shopworn and trite. But there are many other contributions of chemistry and the chemical industry that are equally vital but so subtle and well hidden as to be relatively unknown:

Television, for example, would (mercifully or not, depending upon the point of view) be invisible were it not for 20 cents worth of a luminescent compound that coats the tube and brings the program to visible life.

Twenty-five cents worth of a fluorinated hydrocarbon is all that is necessary to charge the average modern electric refrigerator, with resulting safety and reliability.

The American automobile owner would deplore the use of anything but the modern low-pressure tire. Its use was made possible by the presence in each tire of 8 to 10 cents worth of a chemical antioxidant.

Recently we have learned how to produce silicon metal of exceptional purity and that in turn has made possible a greatly improved transistor. The transistor's tiny bit of silicon, worth about 10 cents, has opened up new vistas in the field of electronics.

Sometimes our research is directed toward a specific goal such as a new fiber, a new plastic, a new paint. More often it is not, and we plow our fields and sow our research seeds hoping and expecting that sufficiently important uses will turn up in other industries to make our effort worth while.

In spite of my distaste for prophecy, I think I can suggest a few important goals for research and particularly chemical research. While I hasten to say I have no idea whether or not they will be reached by 1980, I am quite certain that one day they *will* be reached, be that day in this century or in the next:

It seems to me that only the barest beginning has been made in the use of chemicals for the cure of disease. Today's antibiotics, the sulfa drugs, and anti-malarials, are surely only a hint of what the future will hold. Most illness must be related to body chemistry. What more natural solution than to use chemistry as the corrective agency?

The Slow, Steady Way of Progress

Of greater importance is the maintenance of our body chemistry in good operating condition through proper nutrition. I do not mean here the 2,500 or more calories per day each of us requires as fuel. It is a question rather of a surer and better understanding of the metabolism of the body and the specific chemical processes required to keep it healthy and vigorous. Our knowledge in this area is pathetically small, even though we have progressed far from the "tonic" area. How wonderful it would be if we could include in our diet the figurative ounce-of-prevention that would so well regulate our bodily processes as to make disease a historical curiosity.

There is also the problem of world food supply, which may grow more pressing as the years advance and population increases. Here also chemistry has a role to play through new fertilizers, plant-growth regulants and hormones, pest-control agents, selective weed killers, and veterinary chemicals.

In spite of the extraordinary growth of the plastics industry there is still much to be done in the direction of increasing the utility of plastic products as structural materials. Progress so far has been solid and substantial, but plastics have by no means reached their full stature.

AFTER THE ATOM

There is a final goal, the attainment of which I fear is a long way off, its distance measured in decades rather than in years. How is mankind to supply its ever increasing requirements for energy? By this I mean energy in its broadest sense —not only the energy to drive our turbines, power plants, and automobiles, but the food energy required by the human body.

Over the years many have forecast the exhaustion of our

sources of coal and oil. To be sure, they have all been overly pessimistic, as our supplies of these fuels still seem ample. It seems quite certain, however, that they will indeed be exhausted someday, and it is essential for our survival that we be ready with as good an alternative as possible.

There is much talk these days about atomic energy as the answer to this problem. So it may be, and I have no doubt that we will in due course have central stations powered by the atom. As with coal and oil, however, there is a limit to the earth's supply of fissionable material, and so I am inclined to think that atomic energy, while important, will be only an interim solution.

What we must devise eventually is some way of utilizing more fully the energy that comes to us from the sun. There is a *really* worth-while chain reaction—conveniently placed so one need not fear lethal radiations—generous in its output—and so long-lived that the day of its exhaustion lies in the inconceivably remote future. I wonder what our position would have been today had amounts of money and effort equivalent to those expended on atomic energy been devoted to the utilization of solar energy. Idle speculation—but the solution of the solar-energy problem cannot fail to be of more lasting benefit to mankind.

FUEL IN THE AIR

How the problem will eventually be solved I cannot guess. In the growing of crops, however, we have a technique for the utilization of solar energy that is deficient only in degree. Today the best thermal efficiency we can obtain in growing our crops is perhaps a few tenths of 1 per cent of the energy the sun lavishes on our land. If this could be increased by a factor of ten, the problem of energy and food would be solved for many hundreds of years to come.

The Slow, Steady Way of Progress

The solution seems to depend on some way of hastening, through better utilization of solar energy, the "fixation," if you will, of the carbon dioxide in the atmosphere as burnable, eatable, usable fuel. I say usable advisedly because the chemical industry has a long-term problem too, and that is to supply itself with adequate quantities of organic carbon from which to synthesize not only its present extensive list of products, but those it will develop in the future. We now depend largely upon petroleum and coal, and to a lesser extent on agricultural byproducts. Combustible fuel, organic raw material, and food are all facets of the over-all problem of future energy supply, and no solution is adequate that does not deal with all.

Here then is chemistry's most challenging goal—to devise a biological solar storage battery that, through acceleration of the processes of plant biology, will provide not only energy but food and raw materials as well. I am sure that goal will be reached, not in 1980 but on some fine and glorious day, and in reaching it chemistry will have accomplished its most outstanding task.

CLOISTERED RESEARCH

From all of this you will have gathered that I expect the future to be bright, that there still are goals worth striving for, and that in reaching them chemistry as a science and as an industry will play an important part. None of this, however, can happen automatically, and there are qualifications— two of them, in fact—of substantial and controlling import for future progress.

The first qualification is simple and straightforward. It is that this nation must have a balanced research program, which means that it must supplement its applied research with an amount of fundamental research sufficient to pro-

vide the basic information upon which all scientific progress depends. We define fundamental research as inquiry into
the fundamentals of nature without specific commercial objective. A substantial amount of such research is now being
done by industry. The major responsibility, however, must
rest with our universities, for only they can provide the atmosphere in which truly fundamental scientific inquiry can
properly flourish. The problem is not so much one of per-
suasion as of finance; it is here that industry, by supporting
academic fundamental science, can at the same time supply
a public need and feather its own nest.

CARROT'S TRIUMPH

The second qualification that must be attached to our technological progress is more subtle, more difficult to express,
and politically more distasteful. It is simply that an atmosphere must be provided in this nation within which there
will be incentives of all kinds to persuade men to exercise
in highest degree the talents they possess.

I doubt that there has been any time throughout recorded
history when advances in man's material well-being have
been made so rapidly and so consistently as in our country
during the past two hundred years. Americans have been
accused of being gross materialists, of thinking more of
things and possessions than of ideas and ideals. It has always
seemed to me that there has been a strong element of sour
grapes in those accusations. I doubt very much that there is
any inherent difference between Americans and citizens of
other countries in terms of their material desires. The difference seems to me simply one of the extent to which those
goals have been attained.

I doubt that our progress can be ascribed, except in part,
to our large land area or to our natural resources. What we

have had has been freedom, and, through freedom, the incentive to aspire to any heights we felt we could reach, and when there to reap and to hold the rewards of our accomplishment. We have witnessed over nearly two centuries the inherent virtue of the carrot as compared with the stick.

WHY MONEY?

But in looking toward 1980, we should realize that in recent years we have seriously impaired the incentive of financial reward, principally through our system of extreme progressive personal taxation. I hold no brief for money per se. It is a nice thing to have, in quantities large or small, not because one sits and admires it, like Midas, but because of the constructive things it enables one to do.

We have today an unexcelled network of private universities and schools built up over many years by private beneficence. A large part of our cultural activities—our symphony orchestras, art galleries, museums, libraries, and public gardens—are in being today because individuals with fortunes, large and small, have put them there. Just as these activities have shared the gains of enterprise, they must, perforce, share the losses as taxation shrinks the means of their benefactors.

As to investment, we have in Washington the paradox of a tenderness toward small business together with a system of taxation that effectively removes risk capital from the small enterprise whose need is greatest. The people who would be able and willing to back with risk capital their belief in a modern Henry Ford or Thomas Edison have become a vanishing breed. I have often wondered how many men of genius there are today whose bright ideas have gone into limbo for lack of a backer with courage and at the same time with money he could afford to lose.

Perhaps these are minor questions, inasmuch as they deal

109

only with the question of what one does with money once earned. The more important loss is the loss of the incentive that is based, as it is for so many people, upon material desire. This is an area where business is particularly vulnerable.

Business has traditionally, and by its very nature, depended primarily upon financial reward for accomplishment. It has never had the need to find such non-financial coin as prestige or power to reward its outstanding men. If we agree that the heart of a successful business is sound and able management, then loss of the incentives that have proved attractive must inevitably diminish the chances of satisfactory progress.

ALLURE AT THE SUMMIT

While I may heave a mild sigh of sympathy, I do not worry too much about the senior executives of today. I think that they will do their best quite regardless of the extent to which the tax collector has his way with them. They have been in their jobs long enough to be moved by considerations of obligation, tradition, and loyalty. It is the future that concerns me. For unless business can offer the hope of financial reward I do not see an alternative that will tempt in sufficient numbers the men and women who will fill our upper management ranks a generation or so in the future. The problem arises not so much for mature people, it has its beginnings in earliest manhood. For we must persuade young people, first to put enough effort and thought into their jobs to develop and display their potential, second to accept more responsible positions when offered, and finally to embrace the devotion and single-mindedness that are necessary to make positions of top responsibility effective.

The important thing for our nation's future is to ensure in so far as possible that every one of its people will do the utmost of which he is capable in whatever field of activity he selects. To that end we should have available every incentive ingenious minds can devise. And it seems to me a great catastrophe when financial incentive, traditionally one of the most persuasive, is allowed to fall by the wayside.

TAX BEAUTY?

To be sure, financial reward is only one mark of accomplishment. There are many others, but thus far it is only the financial that has been subjected to the attrition and the arthritis of "progressive" taxation. I can only hope that the tax collector of the future will not discover ways to levy upon the less divisible inducements and satisfactions of life.

Think, for example, how distressing it would be if some of our more spectacularly beautiful females were required to wear veils or other concealing garments in order not to appear more beautiful than their less fortunate sisters. Or suppose Messrs. Heifetz and Menuhin were required to play slightly off key or to pass 91 per cent of their technique on to their less able contemporaries. Or if Professor Linus Pauling were asked to share in some way yet to be devised 91 per cent of the prestige associated with his Nobel Prize with his less able scientific associates.

If these possibilities appear preposterous, let us only reflect that they are nothing more than the extension of current tax philosophies into non-financial areas. And, if we can regard money as only one of the rewards of man, we can see, I think, the inequity of singling it out for special treatment.

I make no pretensions as a tax authority. My only contention is that in levying any tax we should place it in such a way as to be the least possible burden on the growth of the economy. In my opinion the steep ascent of personal taxation slows down the advance of the economy to a degree far overbalancing the revenue collected in the process.

The development of our economy will depend, in the future as in the past, on individual personal achievement. Anything that furthers this end is good business—and wise government. Prestige, public approbation, spiritual satisfaction, financial reward—we need them all, not because we are concerned about the individual recipient but because a nation's progress is in direct proportion to its people's willingness to strive and struggle for whatever goal seems good to them. If we are successful in recapturing that atmosphere of freedom, incentive, and self-respect, the future will be boundless indeed.

GEORGE M. HUMPHREY
Secretary of the Treasury

When George Magoffin Humphrey left Cleveland's $250-million
M. A. Hanna Co. to become Secretary of the Treasury in 1953,
he was probably the least-known member of Dwight Eisenhower's
Cabinet. Today the sixty-five-year-old lawyer-turned-industrialist
from Saginaw, Michigan, is often described as the "strong man"
of the Eisenhower Cabinet.

114

The Future: Sound as a Dollar

BY GEORGE M. HUMPHREY

It is easy to be too conservative when we think about the kind of world we will be living in twenty-five years from now. If we project recent trends, we are likely to picture 1980 merely as a "souped-up" version of 1955. This can be misleading. For the really significant features of 1980 are likely to be the unpredictable contrasts with the present rather than the similarities. If we picture ourselves back in 1930 trying to form an idea of the world of 1955, we can readily see how a conservative approach would have led us astray. Who, twenty-five years ago, could possibly have predicted the vast changes that have taken place in the world's political and economic structures; who could have foreseen the fantastic developments in electronics, antibiotics, or atomic energy?

I have always been skeptical about flat economic predictions; our economy is a sensitive and complex mechanism and any one of a thousand factors can affect its behavior. So I would like to base this look at the coming quarter-century on certain assumptions. There are, after all, some factors in the outlook that seem reasonably predictable even though they can't be projected exactly—the growth of population, the quickening rate of technological development, the rise in productivity and employment, the steady improvement in living standards. Assuming these basic trends, we should give them every encouragement in the years ahead. We must aim not

115

just to maintain but to accelerate the favorable trends of the present. We can't possibly control all the factors bearing on the future, but we can work toward helping the world of 1980 become the kind of world we would like to see.

CHECK LIST FOR CONFIDENCE

A goal that may overshadow all others in importance to our nation is the maintenance of confidence—living, enthusiastic confidence both for today and for the future. It must be shared by everyone—businessmen, workers, investors, and consumers alike. It must be contagious confidence and it must also be practical and justifiable. With such confidence, our nation can move to new heights of production and services, create new and better jobs, and constantly push ahead on a sound basis to an ever finer future.

The confidence displayed in 1954 by American citizens was a main reason the economic readjustment was not more serious. Consumers ignored the gloomy predictions of some economic forecasters and went on to spend more money than ever before. Investors kept making risk capital available. Businessmen went boldly ahead with development and expansion plans. They put large sums in plant, equipment, and research with the firm objective of improving their competitive positions in future years.

All of this helped to create new jobs, to raise incomes, and to advance the nation's productive capacity. It enabled the economy to meet the needs of our growing population and was an eloquent demonstration of the life-giving role confidence can play in a free-enterprise economy.

How can this essential confidence be maintained and strengthened during the next twenty-five years? We shall have to keep working at it all the time. What is required most of all, I believe, is that people develop assurance on the following five major points. They must be convinced:

1. That their government is working fervently—and successfully—for the blessings of lasting peace.
2. That the management of government is in the hands of men of integrity and high moral purpose.
3. That the value of the dollar, with which all transactions are made, will be preserved.
4. That the dynamics of a free competitive economy will be stimulated by government encouragement of private enterprise.
5. That future business declines can and will be held within moderate limits.

I would like to discuss the prospects for the coming quarter-century largely in terms of these basic objectives.

A LESSON TO LEARN

The present high degree of national confidence derives in large part, of course, from the belief that business readjustments now can be kept within tolerably narrow limits, and that, in the future, serious recessions can be avoided. Certainly, events of the recent past have given people new faith in the ability of the government to help moderate economic fluctuations. The fear of a severe recession that was prevalent in 1954 has disappeared, and for this the government's monetary and fiscal policies can take partial credit. Will the next twenty-five years justify the belief that economic adjustments can be kept within reasonable bounds? I happen to believe that if we continue to pursue flexible and sensible financial policies the current optimism may prove to be warranted.

One major lesson concerning recessions is still too little understood, however. We have learned that when business begins to slacken—as a result of excessive inventory accumulation, overbuying by consumers, or for any other reason—an easy credit policy is helpful. The lesson that still needs learning is that credit restraint is equally necessary during periods of expansion, when the seeds of future trouble are sown.

If we are to reach 1980 with our confidence undiminished, and with the economy continuing to operate at highest efficiency, restraints on credit may be needed just as often as easings of credit. This is something to be expected, to live with, and to take into account in making business plans. In this way the government can help diminish the maladjustments and excesses responsible for serious recessions.

A major factor in the maintenance of national confidence is people's confidence in what the dollar is worth. During the decade prior to 1953, the severe decline in the purchasing power of the dollar robbed people of nearly half the value of their savings. This inflation has been brought to a virtual halt, and since 1953 consumers' prices have remained practically unchanged.

We must make sure that the inflationary trends do not reappear. We must work to ensure that the dollar of 1980 will buy at least as much food and clothing as the dollar will buy today—preferably and properly more. If that is done, all will share the benefits of increased productivity, and the saver who puts away a dollar for his retirement, to buy a house, to educate his children, for an emergency, or for any other purpose, will still have a dollar that is worth a dollar when he needs it.

THE STAKE IN STABILITY

This goal of a sound dollar has gained tremendously in importance during the past half-century. This nation, since

1900, has gone through an economic transformation that far exceeds any other in the long history of man's efforts to achieve a better life. The U.S. today is a nation made up, overwhelmingly, of small-to-medium savers and investors. It is a nation of "haves" rather than a nation of "have-nots."

Since the turn of the century real income per man, woman, and child in the U.S. has tripled. And the lower and middle income groups have received the greatest share of this increased income. Early in the century, only ten out of every 100 American families earned as much as $4,000 a year in terms of today's prices; now fifty-five do. Most families now have enough money not only to live adequately, but to save besides. That is the basic economic development that has enabled this country to reach fantastic heights of material prosperity as compared with the rest of the world.

The flow of small savings into an ever broadening investment stream during the past fifty years has been truly remarkable. Ownership by individuals in life-insurance policies has increased from under $2 billion in 1900 to more than $80 billion today. Small investors' holdings of U.S. savings bonds now total nearly $50 billion. More than 10 per cent of all families today own stock in American corporations. Whereas in 1900 individuals had liquid savings amounting to less than $10 billion, now such savings total more than $225 billion.

You can see from these few examples what has been happening to the individual and the family in our wonderland economy. The "average" man in America has acquired a financial stake in the future such as no other "average" citizen anywhere ever had before. We need a completely new set of standards in thinking about ourselves and in defining the "general interest." This nation's economy has grown right over, and left in the dust, both Socialism and Communism.

FROM THE BOTTOM UP

We all want the great beneficial development of the past half-century continued in the next quarter-century—and in many quarter-centuries beyond that. But the progress won't be continued unless we follow national policies that allow the healthy advance of the day-to-day process of "betterment from the bottom up." By this I mean not only policies that will safeguard individual savings against the corroding effect of inflation but also policies that will encourage investment in job-creating plant and equipment and ensure rising production and employment, and so prosperity for our ever growing population.

Confidence that the value of the dollar will be maintained in the next quarter-century will encourage the investment necessary to finance the power and tools for the economic development of the next twenty-five years. The total of the small sums deposited in savings banks, insurance companies, investment trusts, savings and loan associations, pension funds, and other financial institutions will become the large investment to build America.

UNDER NEW MANAGEMENT

To maintain a sound dollar in the years ahead we must continue the sound and flexible monetary and fiscal policies the Eisenhower Administration has been following. Our methods of strengthening confidence in the dollar have been simple. We are steadily curtailing unessential federal spending. And we are increasing the efficiency of government operations.

Cuts in federal expenditures enabled us to travel two-thirds of the way toward a balanced budget in fiscal 1954. And in fiscal 1956, net budget expenditures will be an estimated $11.9 billion below the postwar peak spending of 1953.

We have cooperated with the Federal Reserve Board to assure a smooth meshing of the government's debt-management and monetary policies. While the Federal Reserve Board has used flexible credit and monetary actions to see that the nation's supply of money and credit was kept in line with the needs of the economy, the Treasury has worked toward making the $278-billion federal debt less inflationary and less of a threat to the soundness of the currency.

The Eisenhower Administration inherited a public debt heavily weighted in short-term obligations (the average maturity of the debt in January, 1953, was less than four years). Since short-term debt can add substantially to inflationary pressures (even at times approaching the liquidity of printed money), we have taken action at every appropriate time during the last two years to extend the maturity of the debt by issuing intermediate and long-term securities.

In February, 1955, the Treasury offered a forty-year 3 per cent bond, the longest-term security offered by the Treasury since 1911. The 1995 maturity date was chosen to give the bond wide appeal to such long-term investors as pension trusts and insurance companies. It was designed to supply a real need for a Treasury issue in an area beyond the primary demand for mortgage funds. Long-term investment money was available, and the economic situation permitted long-term refunding of this essentially neutral type without danger of unsettling the economy.

If in the next twenty-five years we use proper opportunities to lengthen the average maturity of the federal debt when we can do so without disrupting the money markets unduly, we can hope that 1980 will find us with a federal debt better balanced than at present as between short, intermediate, and long-term issues, and widely distributed among various classes of investors. We can devoutly hope also that the total amount of the federal debt will be somewhat smaller than at present.

A SMALLER TAX BITE

What about federal tax policy? Within the next twenty-five years it is possible that the threat of Communist imperialism will be reduced to such an extent that we can substantially reduce national security spending. This would give us a long-sought opportunity to lighten substantially the federal tax burden that today consumes nearly a quarter of the total national income. This objective is continually before us. For a cut in the tax share of each income dollar—the maximum cut consistent with the requirements of national defense—would do much to encourage individual initiative and economic growth.

In spite of heavy defense spending, we have already been able to reduce taxes. Sizable cuts in government expenditures made possible a tax reduction in 1954 of $7.4 billion, the largest dollar cut in our history. Moreover, the broad revision of the Internal Revenue Code brought long-needed improvements in the federal tax structure. Much remains to be done, but the 1954 Revenue Act removed many of the inequities and hardships for individuals that had crept into the tax laws over the years, and reduced some of the worst tax hindrances to business incentive. Thus our tax program to date has not only smoothed the 1954 transition from a high to a lower level of government spending but has helped provide a more favorable climate for economic growth over the long run.

In the next quarter-century we must continue working in the direction of reduced taxation. And we must do so in ways that will not only take a smaller percentage of our total national income but in ways that will most encourage the initiative and enterprise which are the very foundation of our economic progress.

GLOBAL GOALS

Another important goal for the next quarter-century should be the strengthening of our economic relationships with other free countries, that we may all prosper together and together build increasingly strong barriers against Communist imperialism.

Efforts to improve economic output here and in other free countries have particular significance in view of the prospect for a rapid increase in world population. By 1980 the U.S. population of 164 million may be increased to well over 200 million; the population of the world, now about 2.5 billion, will exceed three billion at the present rate of increase. The U.S. population growth will affect our entire economic life. It will require more plants and homes and stores and may change the whole face of urban and rural America.

A 20 per cent rise in world population will press increasingly upon the world's land resources and food supplies, and will influence many foreign economic and political problems. It will undoubtedly bring increasing demands for more efficient methods of providing food and other necessities for the people of the world and will provide exceptional opportunities for the application of modern technical knowledge and methods to the production of food, clothing, and other consumer goods.

WHOSE ALLY IS TIME?

Contrary to the popular view, I believe time is working in our favor in the cold war against Communism. As we build up the strength of free people throughout the world, we are erecting barriers to the spread of Communist doctrine. As the free nations are able progressively to improve the welfare of their people, to promote individual freedom and initiative, to raise living standards, improve transportation and communication, encourage international trade, the Communist countries will find themselves operating under increasingly severe handicaps.

The present and future of free-world people look good. An America of confidence, prudence, and imagination will mean that free men of 1980 will see a present—and a future—finer than our minds of today can even dream.

ADLAI E. STEVENSON

Adlai Stevenson, who received the third-largest popular vote in
U.S. history (second biggest: F.D.R. in 1936) is once again a
presidential candidate. He is now practicing law in Chicago—a
profession that has occupied him off and on since 1952. In 1953
he dropped in on thirty nations in a six-month trip around the
world; in 1955 he visited Africa.

Stevenson stands as one of the country's foremost political
leaders, and the Democratic party's most eloquent spokesman.
His Democratic heritage is deep. His grandfather, Adlai I, was
a Vice President of the U.S. under Cleveland, and later an unsuccessful running mate of William Jennings Bryan. In 1933
Adlai Stevenson II began his own career in government as a
lawyer in the New Deal's AAA. Fifteen years of intermittent
service in various agencies and missions of the Roosevelt and
Truman administration were climaxed by his surprising and
runaway election, in 1948, as governor of Illinois.

My Faith in Democratic Capitalism

BY ADLAI E. STEVENSON

I am invited by the editors to look forward with them toward 1980 and to join in the suggestion of goals for American achievement during the next quarter-century. The ultimate goals are, of course, very clear: peace, freedom for ourselves as individuals, and a realization of Man's place in a meaningful scheme of things. But it is to a narrower focus that I am asked to address myself: namely, the future of the relationship between two great forces in America's structure —the force of business and industry on the one hand, and on the other, the force of government, particularly the federal government.

If it is expected that comment on this subject by one sometimes close to government—particularly a Democrat!—must inevitably be antagonistic and critical, and slanted against "Big Business," I promise disappointment. I think of this relationship between business and government as essentially one of cooperation between two institutional forces wholly dependent upon each other. If there were but one twenty-five-year goal to fix upon in this area it would be, for me, to stop the talk about a basic antagonism between American business and government, and replace such nonsense with a recognition of the common purposes and obligations of these two cornerstones of democratic capitalism.

We all make the mistake of thinking about institutions, such as business and government, as ends in themselves. Most of the friction between businessmen and bureaucrats in this country has arisen from their constantly having to remind each other that neither government nor business is an end in itself, that they both are only institutional means to the ends of individual purpose; and that whether the relationship between them is "good" or "bad" is measurable solely in terms of how the relationship pays off in the lives and satisfactions of 165 million people, or, more broadly, of all humanity.

I find the measure of the strength of this relationship in the fact that the past quarter-century has seen in America the most extraordinary growth any nation or civilization has ever experienced. Our rise in population has been largely a function of our increased prosperity and productivity; our millions of new mouths to feed are better fed than fewer mouths were only twenty-five years ago. The possessions of a modest family today exceed those of a "prosperous" one in 1930. While the population of some unhappy countries rises against the most dreadful counterpressures and in spite of wishes that it could be restrained, our numbers increase out of a sense that we can well afford such increase. An important part of the example we show the world is the fact that we are the nation of the most powerful consumers on earth.

OLD SNARLING RITUALS

It was not always so. It was not so twenty-five years ago. It is a curious thing that the two institutional forces in the democratic capitalistic society that contributed most directly to this emergence of the powerful consumer during this quarter-century seemed to snarl at each other every step of their common way. The bounding prosperity of postwar America has been due in large measure to processes in which government and business have in effect played complementary and cooperative roles. The New Deal legislation of the Thirties helped to provide a "built-in" consumer demand that business could then work to satisfy, and the increase of 70 per cent in the scale of the American economy between 1939 and 1944 was achieved by the closest cooperation between government and industry in America's war effort.

Yet, in spite of this practical realization of common interests and common goals, it became part of the ritual of New Deal politics to castigate a business system that has always been recognized by Americans as the only permanent source of the jobs and consumer purchasing power which "the government" was trying to restore. And in the meantime the businessmen, who rose from prostration to record-breaking prosperity through satisfying a multi-billion consumer demand that was stimulated and buttressed by New Deal legislation, became the bitterest critics of this New Deal legislation.

I know the arguments that business *might* have recovered even faster in the later Thirties if it hadn't been for government "regimentation" (also referred to as "drift") and "exercise of arbitrary power" (also referred to as "indecisiveness"). If those arguments ever needed answer they have it in the decision of the present "businessman's government" in Washington not to curtail the federal programs that underwrite consumer purchasing power but to enlarge them. Nor in current talk of "getting government out of business" does there appear to be much recognition that government is in business to the tune of about $15 billion worth of military orders each year and is therefore playing, whatever the theory of the matter, a decisive part in keeping demand steady through the whole economy.

One of the future goals for American government and American business must surely be a fuller recognition that the maintenance of demand in the interests of the consumer—which is one of the few things everybody in this country is—is basic to both.

OUR NEW COMMONALITY

A broader aspect of the common purpose of business and government in America emerges from recognition of the new and tremendous sense of commonality that has come over this nation in the past twenty-five years. The individual no longer stands alone. His smallest community is larger, and more diverse in its services. His light and power come no longer from his own windmill or from some small local utility company, but usually from a vast network. His bank is strongly interconnected with its fellows, and his deposits are insured. The same news reaches him and his neighbors, and faster than it ever did before. An incredible linkage of wires and roads and cooperative enterprises, public and private, has taken isolation (and now isolationism) from all but the remotest homes in America.

In ways we hardly realize, this commonality brings inevitable interweavings of the functions of business and government. When the services of even two people are joined there are decisions of "governing" to be made; and when thousands and then millions invest or work together in a common business enterprise, their dealings together become more and more like the relationships we call government. What we used to think of as the "decentralized decision-making of the market place" has given way to various processes of large-scale private institutional decision-making remarkably like that of government in both its methods and its results. We constantly see in such things as labor unions, corporations, and trade associations, and in the "bargaining" that goes on between them, a reflection of the private institutional needs for "government."

My Faith in Democratic Capitalism

As a people we are doing world-shaking and history-making things today—partly as the result of individual genius, but perhaps even more because we have learned of the powers of individuals working together. A brilliant professor turned businessman, Beardsley Ruml (who reformed the nation's thinking on how to collect the income tax and has more recently been trying to perform an equal miracle on our notion of the federal budget), has declared that the greatest economic discovery of the twentieth century so far is the realization that the wisely directed actions of all of us, *as a whole,* can compensate for the aberrations or misfortunes of a few. A. J. Toynbee suggests that three hundred years from now the twentieth century will be remembered, not for its wars, not for its conquests of distance and disease, not even for the splitting of the atom—but for "having been the first age, since the dawn of civilization, some five or six thousand years back, in which people dared to think it practicable to make the benefits of civilization available for the whole human race." I hope the judgment of this great historian comes true. My instincts tell me it will.

It was in America that the first practical stirrings of this great idea began. We must bring the idea to such perfection that it will save the very civilization it has awakened. Another goal, then, for 1980 America—so that we may disprove George Orwell's terrifying prediction for 1984—is that this process of our growing commonality must and will be everywhere recognized and acknowledged, *not so that it can be senselessly accelerated, but so that it can be wisely guided and controlled.* I hold no belief in economic determinism; I bow to Shakespeare, not Marx, when I declare that there is a tide in the affairs of men, and that we had better acknowledge it.

THE ARMY OF MASS MEDIOCRITY

This new sense of commonality is not without its dangers. Security, whether economic, political, or social, has become an individual and national obsession. I wonder if we fully realize the relationship between this yearning for security and the problem of maintaining our civil liberties. Security doesn't come free. Sometimes its price—or the price some would charge for it—is conformity and groupthink, and so it becomes part of the future joint obligation of the forces of business and government to respect, yes and protect, those elements of individuality that commonality threatens.

It is not true that the individual rolls around today like a kernel of grain between the upper and nether millstones of Big Government and Big Business—but there is a danger here that is great enough to warrant our keeping such a picture always in mind. Even as we become increasingly vigilant in our battle against the debilitating force of Communism we must be aware of another enemy that creeps upon us even more quietly and insidiously: the army of mass mediocrity, with banners flying.

Democracy's literature is full of warnings against the overpowering of the individual by the agencies of government and business. A hundred years ago John Stuart Mill deplored society's encroachments on the individual. John Ruskin prophesied the destruction of aesthetics by the industrial revolution. Lord Acton used some of his careful, rationed counsel to warn that democracy's flaw might prove to be—despite its protestations of the state's sublimation to the individual—a lack of moral criteria. Learned, sensitive, eloquent, these eminent Victorians voiced their concern that progress in the arts of statecraft and industry might make its intended beneficiaries its victims. Perhaps our survival in the face of these unhappy prophecies shows how wrong they were. Surely the individual is still today not *wholly* fenced in, except by the Kremlin, which Mill did not happen to be thinking of. As for the destruction of aesthetics, it turns out that in some ways—in modern design, in support of artistic efforts—industry is one of the best friends aesthetics has in the modern world.

I STAND WITH COOLIDGE...

Yet we know, from warnings that are more sensed than seen or heard, that all is not well with our status as individuals. Consciously or unconsciously, we are erecting battlements against our own accomplishments. Man in the individual sense today is not Man's only adversary. We are concerned, too, about a strange, not wholly definable force in which there are at least the identifiable elements of "government" and "technology" and "massiveness" in this age of mass population, mass education, mass communications—yes, and mass manipulation. Indeed it seems that at mid-twentieth century, mass manipulation is a greater danger to the individual than was economic exploitation in the nineteenth century; that we are in greater danger of becoming robots than slaves. Surely it is part of the challenge of this next quarter-century that industry and government and the society they both support must find new and better ways of restoring scope to that strange eccentric, the individual.

Nostalgia won't help. We shall never dis-invent the airplane, which sets down the evil of Communism in our backyard instead of leaving it to fester outside our notice five thousand miles away. We shall never recover the quiet privacy the individual had before the telephone, the hand camera, and the microphone. We shall not relock the atom. A small fraction of our citizens have already come out flatly for government by lie-detector. Some businesses maintain, in the name of security, "black lists" that in effect can deprive a man of the right to work without inquiry, due process, or even hope of ultimate redress. I can't help suspecting that some social scientists and even psychiatrists would love to find a combination of electronic devices by which every citizen could be measured for the slightest personal or social aberrations from some assigned "norm," and I suspect they will get it from our onrushing technologists. On this kind of assault on the individual I stand precisely where Calvin Coolidge stood on sin: I am agin it. I propose to keep on being agin it.

MOBILITY IS NOT FREEDOM

But we shall have to learn the art of coexistence with many strange things in the future, some of them perhaps even stranger than Communism. Technology, while adding daily to our physical ease, throws daily another loop of fine wire around our souls. It contributes hugely to our mobility, which we must not confuse with freedom. The extensions of our senses, which we find so fascinating, are not adding to the discrimination of our minds, since we need increasingly to take the reading of a needle on a dial to discover whether we think something is good or bad, or right or wrong.

Deepest pride in the accomplishments of America's inventive genius is no warrant for congratulating ourselves on any best-of-all-possible-worlds. Materially we can—and will—do better still. But spiritually, morally, and politically, I don't think we are doing so well. Both industry and government are contributing enormously to the almost unbelievable advance of technology in America—but both must become increasingly aware of their moral and spiritual responsibilities. The representative of a great manufacturing concern, speaking about the phenomenon we call automation, concluded: "I don't think it is the part, nor can it be the part, of industry to try to plan the social aspects of this thing." It seems to me, to the contrary, that industry is eventually, with government, going to have to do its full share of thinking about the sociology as well as the economics of such things as automation and the split atom. The more realistic and broad-gauge view is suggested by David Sarnoff's comment, in an earlier chapter, that "if freedom is lost, if the dignity of man is destroyed, advances on the material plane will not be 'progress' but a foundation for a new savagery."

WE LISTEN TO BUSINESSMEN

There is increasing realization that one of the biggest problems of these next twenty-five years will be what we are going to do with "the new leisure" which it appears will develop as one of the fruits of the new technology. As people learn how to live longer after their service in the regular work force is done, as machines and "feedbacks" and push buttons take on more and more of the job of production, as the inevitably shortened work week materializes—with these things there comes a whole host of new adjustments to be made. No one need fear the long-range effects of machines replacing men, but the adjustment is going to require responsible and thoughtful administration, and the new leisure will mean new happiness only if care is taken not to confuse leisure with just plain having nothing to do.

It is inevitable that government in America will be called upon during this next quarter-century to meet the social implications of these ever more rapid technological advances, and I see no reason why American industry should not participate fully and freely in this enterprise. There seems to me no escape from this obligation. It just will not do to leave all worrying about our souls to the educators, the clergy, and the philosophers. The men to whom mass-America tunes its ear today are businessmen—indeed, they seem to have more influence on youth than the schools, more influence on the devout than the clergy, more influence on the wicked than the thought of perdition. With this prestige goes a responsibility that can be given no artificial boundaries.

I shall not attempt to suggest a particular role for industry in the transforming of technology's dark threats into bright promises. Part of this role will undoubtedly lie in an increased laying aside of great funds to foster education in all fields, not confining such funds to the sciences or to what is of immediate or "practical" significance. The day of the great individual philanthropist is nearly over, and industry must step into this breach. Even as I write this there comes to my desk a list of fifty research memoranda being prepared as part of a joint project of a large private corporation and a branch of the federal government. Would that just one of the fifty memoranda related to the heart of industrial progress—instead of all of them to its hands and feet and muscle! Adolf A. Berle Jr. suggests in his recent book a broader emergent concept of the corporation as an instrument of social leadership and responsibility, chargeable with a stewardship as broad as all the implications of its economic effects. This, it seems to me, must be the direction of our progress.

WHO CREATED AMERICA?

It could be hoped that one of the dividends of a "businessman's government" might be a merging of the thinking *both* in business and in government about economic and human affairs. And yet there has been quite a lot of talk from high government spokesmen about being "conservative" in economic affairs and "liberal" in human affairs. I don't know how

136

this works where something like unemployment or social security is involved. Are those "economic" or "human" affairs?

If there is value in a definition of "conservatism" that would cross economic-human and business-government lines (and even Republican-Democratic lines), may I reiterate what Thomas Carlyle said a hundred years ago: the conservatism that *really* conserves is that which lops off the dead branch to save the living tree. Our American economy has fewer dead branches than that of any other nation, I am sure; but that we shall need pruning and spraying and the application of new fertilizers and growth regulators in the future as in the past, I have no doubt. Should it perhaps be part of our purpose in these years ahead to recognize that the process of conservation must be a joint government and business responsibility, and that division of function between "human" and "economic" is unrealistic in today's complex society?

I hope this quarter-century will see a frank recognition that every new frontier in American progress has been, and will always be, opened up by the *joint* enterprise of business and government. Great respect for the concept of the "rugged individualist" (usually incorporated) is no warrant for the illusion that modern America was *created* by businessmen—any more than it was by Senators or the Founding Fathers. Before colonial America could emerge from its colonialism, and a few cities could become interconnected with a subsistence agriculture and the tinkering sheds of a few ingenious Yankees, the federal government had to assert its power. Before America could become a great industrial nation the federal government had to assert its power over territory in terms of a U.S. Army that would explore and protect; in terms of a federal treasury that would regulate and expand the national credit; and in many other terms of a state that would hold title to the whole public domain until private entrepreneurs could slowly, on terms adjudged to be for the public benefit, take over vital business and industrial procedures. There were very few businessmen (and no government officials) in the Conestoga wagons that toiled across the West only a little more than a century ago; their time and place and function came later.

No; business did not create America or the American way. The American way was created in a complex collaboration whereby the federal government offered to individuals the best soil and nurture for enlightened capitalism ever devised—and the individuals took it on the generous terms offered.

WASHINGTON MUST HELP

Nor is this interdependence of government and business reflected only in historical vignettes. We accept today as one of our great principles that operation of industry is a properly private function. Yet so long as technology burgeons, the interrelationships between government and industry will continue to grow more complex, not less. Where technology disemploys workers, government will be asked to help. It must help. Where it creates surpluses, government will be asked to help. It must help.

There is no reason to be afraid of growing complexity; indeed our option is to deal cheerfully and courageously with growing complexity—or to go over the authoritarian abyss. I see no reason why the need to confront complexity is more ominous merely because it may require new formulas of private-public cooperation.

A fascinating future relationship between government and business, for example, will occur when Alaska is truly "opened." Before business and industry can begin to pour Alaska's resources into the mainstream of the world's commercial life, millions of dollars worth of trunk and access roads

138

will have to be built, and someone will have to complete the geological mapping of 586,400 square miles of territory so that private mining companies will have some notion of what, where, and how great the mineral treasure of Alaska really is —facts unknown today. Shall we organize a purely private Alaskan Corporation of America to take all these risks? Or may it be necessary to accept some subvention from the federal government to get things going? Regardless of our preachments we may be sure it will be the latter, as in large part it already has been.

In spite of resounding keynote speeches and business-convention oratory, it is an obvious fact that this pattern of cooperation between government and private enterprise runs through our economy from end to end. One of the most pervasive of all influences is without doubt the tariff—that massive governmental intervention that is generally left off the standard anathema list of many businessmen. Much of the work of the Atomic Energy Commission is undertaken through the agency of private corporations. Business in the Northwest has certainly not been retarded by cheap public power. And just how much of the newspaper and magazine industry is carried by the taxpayer through the government's massive subsidy of second-class mail?

There will be a testing of a good deal of unthinking talk when it comes time to consider translating into action the Hoover Commission's recommendations for liquidating the structure of government lending agencies. It seems a conservative prognosis that these recommendations will be loudly honored for their expression of the sacrosanct and sound principle of the least-government-possible and that it will then be more quietly decided that most of these agencies (with perhaps a little exterior redecoration) come within the least-possible limits.

ADLAI E. STEVENSON

IS GOVERNMENT "CREEPING"?

I am not suggesting that American business and industry owe either an unpaid debt or any attitude of servile gratitude to the federal government. The creative record of American capitalism is altogether too strong and dignified in its own right to call for subservience to any other force. What I am suggesting, however, is that there could be a good deal more realism and quite a lot less nonsense in the recognition by the business community of the interdependence, if you will, of the two essential democratic capitalistic institutions of business and government. We are past the point of adolescence in a relationship where it once was perhaps understandable that those who profited in largest sum from the operation of our system of things might still clamor about the federal government as a childishly operated nuisance, which hampers business, which intrudes, which confiscates or expropriates profits, and in a thousand ways spoils all the fun and is constantly threatening to "socialize" all America by creeping. It seems to me an essential element of present maturity to recognize that the relationships between the two institutions do not consist exclusively of government's recourseless taxation or browbeating of business.

We too rarely realize how very great and needless a strain is placed on this relationship just by the verbal violence that is indulged in in describing its elements. "Economic royalists" was an unfair and unfortunate epithet. To call the TVA "Communism," or rural electrification "Socialism"—the list of such clichés is long—is a kind of nonsense that insults the facts and serves only evil. It is an important goal for America-1980 that what is publicly said or reported regarding such things be better adjusted to what is generally true. This will

140

require, among other things, an enormous improvement in the standards and practices of American journalism.

FREER AND FREER TRADE

Before leaving the subject of the interaction of government and industry, I should speak of a vital area in which failure to formulate joint and consistent policies can have the effect not simply of weakening the domestic economy but of imperiling America's position of leadership in the free world. I refer, of course, to those tariff, trade, and custom practices that hamper and addle world commerce to the disadvantage of the whole Western world, ourselves included. As a goal for the future, to be achieved many years sooner than distant 1980, I would certainly hope for relaxed restrictions on world commerce—a relaxation not just on tariffs—to the end of freer and freer trade among the nations. Policies that were appropriate only in the day when it was accurate to speak of "our infant industries" can lead to social, political, and economic misfortune in our industrial manhood. And insofar as the need for capital and technical assistance in the less developed areas has become perhaps the greatest limiting factor on expanding world trade, I would hope, too, for new and courageous action by public and private agencies in this field as well. On tariff reductions the government (under Democratic administrations, at least) has led the way since 1934 and earlier. In providing capital and technical "know-how" for world development, it is the government that has made the start. Business must educate its members to follow.

A SPIRAL IN THE OFFING?

But perhaps the most urgent problem that will be set before government and business alike by pressures generated beyond America's frontier will prove to be the issue of disarmament.

We cannot deny that the overwhelming desire of our own people and of all the world's peoples is to be rid of the nightmare of atomic war. There are some signs that the Communists are feeling this enormous pressure of popular longing for peace. It is not inconceivable that in the next decade we shall be required to take the lead in dismantling a part of our vast military structure of preparedness. The impact upon the national economy of falling expenditures for arms will be profound and it will take the best efforts and the concerted efforts of government and business to see that the transition from a large measure of military spending to an overwhelming civilian economy is accomplished without a downward spiral and grave dislocation in the whole economic system. Neither government nor business can manage that alone. It would be well if its implications were examined jointly—and soon.

Perhaps most of what I have mentioned here comes together in a suggestion that we might profitably think in terms of a doctrine of "separation of powers" in this area of business and government relations—a separation resembling the constitutional differentiation between the executive, the legislative, and the judicial in government itself. This is a formula for "checks and balances," and yet essentially for coordination and cooperative functioning toward common goals. The future of government and business does not consist in *either one* having ambitions to take over the functions of the other. It is an essential goal for the future to keep their separation jealously guarded.

Government in America has *always* regarded the operation of industry as a purely private function. To return to an earlier example, even the newest-biggest of all governmental agencies, born in the early days of the Atomic Age and the Fair Deal—the AEC—operates its vast, complex, "monopolistic," and largely secret domain through private industrial con-

142

tractors. But business has yet to show a comparably broad and tolerant understanding of the legitimate domain of government. In fact, some sections of the business community could not do better than follow, in this regard, Dr. Johnson's advice, and clear their minds of cant and prejudiced misinformation, not to say the downright nonsense about "governmental dictatorship," and, of course, "creeping Socialism" that all too often, as a species of businessmen's groupthink, takes the place of responsible consideration of the proper functions of government in free society.

This idea of a different kind of "separation of powers" does not require being against "businessmen in government." Not at all. But it does suggest that when businessmen, like anyone else, are being selected for government posts, it should be because of their talents for the job of government and for no other reason. To the extent that "businessmen in government" means the introduction into government of the ideals and practices of efficiency for which American business is justly famous—and to the degree that it also means adding to government councils an intimate understanding of industry and commerce—to that extent and degree this is all to the good and none should object. The case is very different, though, wherever a businessman brings with him to government any ideas other than a completely objective and independent concept of the public good.

LAND OF HOPE AND GLORY

An intelligent businessman, now a member of the current Administration, said before he reached his present public eminence: "Commercial interests are not the same as national interests." How right he was, and is. Although commercial interests and national interests can and usually do walk a certain distance hand in hand, no full identity between them can ever be forced, and any attempt to force it would be apt to end in misery, or disaster, or both—and for both.

Over the years, the federal government, in Republican and Democratic administrations, enacted the Sherman and the Clayton acts to prevent concentrations of power in plutocratic hands, and no wiser or more beneficial legislation has ever been enacted in America—for business. In Europe, where these laws are incomprehensible, and a cozy hand-in-glove-ism between governments and industries has its expression in the cartel system, we see many brilliant accomplishments. But we do not see any properly significant diffusion downward of the profits and benefits of the industrial system, which, in this country, constitutes our most effective safeguard against radical infection in any large masses of our public.

It was governmental intervention, beginning about fifty years ago, that broke up the trusts. If American business had remained in the image of the "oil trust," the "steel trust," the "sugar trust," the "whiskey trust," America as we know it today would never have come into existence, and the leadership of the modern world would almost certainly reside elsewhere— doubtless in a totally Prussianized or Communized Europe, with the British Isles reduced to the status of a tourist resort, and America still a giant agricultural bumpkin among the nations.

Events took a very different turn. We are not yet fully grown up to our responsibilities of world leadership, and we groan understandably under the burdens placed upon us. But despite two hideous wars, the history of the twentieth century is by no means so tragic—yet—as it might be, and the vast area of hope still alive in the world lies squarely here, with us. The past interactions between American government and American business, brawling and ill-natured though they were, have been a major determinant of the shape and course of the mod-

144

ern Western world. Given an improved respect and understanding between these properly separated forces in America, I can look forward to the next twenty-five years with confidence, and think of all the Western world, potentially, as a land of hope and glory, Mother of the Free.

"What is past," says the inscription in front of the National Archives Building in Washington, "is prologue." To this I say amen.

ROBERT E. SHERWOOD

The late Robert Emmet Sherwood was a playwright, historian and passionate defender of freedom. Sherwood's first Broadway play, *The Road to Rome,* was produced in 1927; three of his later plays, *Idiot's Delight, Abe Lincoln in Illinois,* and *There Shall Be No Night,* won Pulitzer Prizes. During World War II he left Broadway for Washington, where he helped write President Roosevelt's speeches and served as Director of the Overseas Operation of the OWI. His biography, *Roosevelt and Hopkins* (1948), brought him a fourth Pulitzer Prize, and his movie, *The Best Years of Our Lives* (1946), won nine Academy Awards and the New York Film Critics' Award.

Sherwood once said of himself that he "suffered from Causes." His written words, whether in plays, speeches, or biography, almost always carried a message. Here, in "There Is No Alternative to Peace," his message is a clear and stirring affirmation of the "element of divinity" in mankind, which, he believed, would make the threat of a third world war "a malodorous memory" before 1980.

146

"There Is No Alternative to Peace"

BY ROBERT E. SHERWOOD

It seems self-evident that all prophecy or speculation concerning the next twenty-five years—or the next millennium—must be entirely dependent upon the ability of our own and other nations to prevent calamitous war.

Obviously, we do not allow our apprehensions to overcome our aspirations for the advancement of our spiritual life, economy, education, civil liberties, scientific progress, health and welfare, arts and letters, and everything else that is involved in the perpetual pursuit of happiness; but, equally obviously, we cannot ignore the fact, staring us violently in the face, that the very aspiration to life itself may be blasted any one of these days into radioactive rubble.

President Eisenhower has said, "Since the advent of nuclear weapons, it seems clear that there is no longer any alternative to peace." On another occasion he told the delegates to the United Nations that he could say that "the defense capabilities of the United States are such that they could inflict terrible losses upon an aggressor." But, he continued, "to stop there would be to accept helplessly the probability of civilization destroyed—the annihilation of the irreplaceable heritage of mankind handed down to us generation from generation—and the condemnation of mankind to begin all over again the age-old struggle upward from savagery toward decency and right and justice."

The nuclear weapons are not the only existing giants of annihilation: there are also the appalling instruments of chemical and biological warfare. While the laboratories have continued their unremitting efforts to conquer disease, they have been ominously successful in devising new ways to inflict disease and pollution on entire populations.

And yet, you will encounter some citizens who seem to view the prospect of war as calmly as if there were no essential difference in offensive weapons from the embattled farmer's musket—the musket that "fired the shot heard round the world." You will hear that all we need now is to deliver one Sunday punch. (You will recall that Pearl Harbor happened on a Sunday.) There are orators and writers who tell us that we can win a third world war in anything from three days to three weeks. This easy and horribly delusive assurance is usually expressive of the sentiment which favors some form of "preventive" war, and which is held by some able and honorable men as well as by some irresponsible scoundrels; but it is clearly not the sentiment of the President nor of the people for whom he speaks.

DISARMAMENT, OR ELSE...

There can be small question of doubt that the people of this country, and of the whole civilized world, are more opposed than ever before to war and to any policies and programs that, they fear, might increase the danger of war. Many of them even accept the need for substantial personal sacrifices—compulsory military service, abnormal taxes—as means for the prevention of war. Certainly, if there are politicians who favor dropping the hydrogen bombs now ("beat 'em to the punch")—or other politicians who feel we should cut our own armed forces to the bone ("it's the only way to reduce the income tax")—those politicians would hardly dare to state their real views candidly on any platform from which they must confront the voters.

World disarmament—down to the minimum required by needs of the police forces, whether local or international—is surely as valid as any objective to be hoped for and worked for between now and 1980.

If this objective of disarmament is not achieved by 1980— long before 1980—then we may as well write FINIS to the human story. When we consider what deadly scientific progress has been made in the sixteen years since Albert Einstein wrote a letter to Franklin D. Roosevelt about the potentialities of nuclear fission, we may well be appalled by contemplation of what might be produced during another few years of fierce competition in military preparation between rival nations, rival ideologies. If we have not already reached the ultimate in the capacity for mutual destruction, we shall be reaching it soon.

Is this gross exaggeration? I can only repeat the words of the President: "there is no longer any alternative to peace."

There is a total degree of finality about those considered words.

Very well. What can we do about it? All I can do is express the belief—or, if you will, the faith—that before 1980 the threat of a third world war will be a malodorous memory, existing only on the library shelves, and not on the front pages. If you ask me for convincing reasons for my optimism, I can provide no facts or figures, no blueprints, no statistics or charts or expert analyses. I can say only that my confidence in the future is founded on the fact that I believe in God.

I believe in the assurance, given in the first chapter of the first book of the Bible, that "God created man in his *own* image." (The italics are the Bible's.)

That is the most important statement in the recorded history of the human race. It has provided both the inspiration and the justification of all of man's progress. The essential concept of the divinity that exists in man is the force that impelled man out of the jungle and along the ascending path that leads to the stars. (Even if he never reaches them, it is a wonderful thing that he has been perpetually climbing in that direction, the poor, insignificant, invincible little creature.) His perhaps blind but persistent faith in his godlike qualities has enabled man to defy all scientific proof that he is frail, physically and morally—that he is subject to corruption and decay—that he is, in a word, mortal. He has gone out on his own and found ways to make himself immortal.

It is a cardinal principle of mathematical science that the whole is equal to the sum of its parts. But man has confounded scientific analysis, including the Freudian, because he is demonstrably greater than the sum of his parts. That unknown, uncharted, inexplicable margin is the element of divinity. If we could ever find a way of measuring that margin, differing widely among individuals, we might be able to explain genius, to explain how there ever happened to be a Socrates, Michelangelo, Shakespeare, Newton, Beethoven, Lincoln, Einstein—yes, and Freud himself, and Albert Schweitzer, and Willie Mays.

Thus believing, I find it inconceivable that man is about to destroy himself with the products of his own God-given genius. But—the dreadful fact remains that the suitable weapons are there and available to powerful rulers who have displayed no antagonism to homicide. Therefore it is evident that we must do more than just hope for "the best in the best of all possible worlds." And "we" means everyone. Our national leaders are strong and wise only to the extent that the majority of the people who nominate and elect them are strong and wise. It may be all very well for a stockholder to give his proxy to the organization while the dividends are coming in satisfactorily, but the citizen cannot afford to hand out proxies blindly to his political leaders; behind those proxies must lie long and arduous thought, deliberation and debate; the mandate must be both informed and mature. In this modern age, ignorance is insanity.

Some twenty-four centuries ago an Athenian dramatist, Sophocles, wrote, "When Divine power plans evils for a man, it first injures his mind." Longfellow's variant of the same thought was, "Whom the Gods would destroy they first make mad." The most important weapons in the arsenal of the free world today are still sanity, awareness, understanding, courage, and faith. Another essential quality is patience.

HISTORY DOESN'T REPEAT

The next years will test man's capacity for greatness as it has never been tested before. The issue is sheer survival. If we retain the capacity that has been shown over and over again through all the centuries, we shall survive. If we have lost it, we will never know what hit us.

In a previous chapter General Sarnoff has written, and with high authority, of the seemingly incredible technical advances that man will make in the foreseeable future. He described them with a wonderful phrase: "numberless embryos in the womb of science." And Dr. von Neumann suggests that we shall be able to gain control over the weather—we could extend tropical climate into the Arctic. He writes, "What power over our environment, over all nature, is implied!"

One can hardly accuse Dr. von Neumann of overstatement. If we can control the weather then our powers really are unlimited; we might even learn how to control ourselves.

We suspect that we are advancing cautiously across what has been described by some anonymous soothsayer as "an apparently endless plateau of suspense." It is highly unfamiliar ter-

151

rain for us Americans, and the signposts and beacons, if any, are apt to be utterly misleading, many of them deliberately so.

At times when the present is murky and the future a mass of black thunderclouds with visibility zero, we are naturally inclined to look backward into the past for guidance and even more for reassurance. It is sometimes an easy form of escapism to think that history always repeats itself . . . human nature never changes . . . there is a grand pattern to the events of time and if we study that pattern carefully enough we shall know what next is to be woven by the hand of destiny. I believe that too much reliance on the lessons of history can be highly dangerous. The doctrinaire pronouncement that "it was thus and so yesterday—ergo it will be thus and so tomorrow" can be listed, in the present age of upheaval, under Famous Last Words. The old theories of "rigid determinism," or "historical inevitability," are dead—and, incidentally, those obsolete theories were completely consistent with dogmatic Marxism. I would suggest that the wisest maker of major policy today is one who has learned as much as possible about the past and then has forgotten it—or rather, relegated it to the remote background of his mind so that it is there solely for purposes of illustration at his convenience.

THE CONVENIENT DEVIL THEORY

One of the most damaging delusions that we have suffered from in recent times is the belief, based on historical experience, that "one man and one man only" is responsible for all of our troubles and fears. There was ample reason for that. Napoleon Bonaparte provoked a series of wars that extended all the way from the Nile and the Moskva rivers to the Mississippi. Napoleon's defeat at the battle of Waterloo in 1815 was followed by a century of relative peace. There were local wars

—including one big one, our own Civil War—but there was no serious disruption of the "concert of powers."

About the middle of that century of peace after Waterloo, Charles Darwin wrote: "As all the living forms of life are the lineal descendants of those which lived long before the Cambrian epoch, we may feel certain that the ordinary succession by generation has never once been broken, and that no cataclysm has desolated the whole world. Hence, we may look with some confidence to a secure future of equally inappreciable length. And as natural selection works solely by and for the good of each being, all corporeal and mental environments will tend to progress toward perfection."

Also, about the middle of the marvelous nineteenth century, Victor Hugo wrote: "Give time for the realization of the acme of social salvation—gratuitous and compulsory education. How long will it take? A quarter of a century; and then imagine the incalculable sum of intellectual development . . . Look! raise your eyes! The supreme epic is accomplished. The legions of light drive backward the hordes of flame."

These two preceding quotations were not from starry-eyed idealists, crackpots; Darwin and Hugo possessed two of the greatest minds in an age of extraordinary enlightenment. But —how tragically naive they appear now! A half a century after Victor Hugo expressed his vote of confidence, the "legions of light" were converging to fight the first world war, which proved to be only a rehearsal for the barbarities which were to follow and which have not abated. (And if you are consequently dubious of my own vote of confidence in the next twenty-five years you have, as the French say, reason.)

The convenient theory of "one man and one man only" persisted. The imposing image of Napoleon, glowering down upon civilization from his perch atop the pillar in the Place Vendôme, sustained the illusion that we could solve all of our present, pressing problems by the elimination of Public Enemy No. 1. It was so much more comfortable to ignore the forces that produced him. We shouted "Hang the Kaiser" in 1918, as if that would solve everything, and, in 1945, when the deflated corpse of Adolf Hitler was incinerated in the shattered ruins of Berlin, we believed that all we need to do now is "bring the boys home." Fortunately, we were not similarly stupefied by the death of Josef Stalin, perhaps the most tyrannical and shortsighted of all the dictators. (It is terrifying to contemplate what might have been the consequences if Stalin had been more farsighted, but the word "if" can have no legitimate place in history, being reserved only for romanticists who like to imagine what might have happened if John Wilkes Booth had missed, or if Eve had been repelled by the very sight of a snake.)

THE WORLD REVISED

In his anxiety to avoid repeating the well-intentioned mistakes of Woodrow Wilson, such as the unilateral and premature commitments in the Fourteen Points (which were later to provide prime ammunition for Hitler in his rise to power), Franklin Roosevelt made well-intentioned mistakes of his own; he wanted to make no postwar commitments of any kind until the "Peace Conference" was convened, but time ran out on him, and so did Stalin. As it happened there never was a "Peace Conference" after World War II, which provides further evidence that the seeking of guidance from history can be dangerously misleading.

Regardless of the theory that history always repeats itself, the fact is that the predicament in which we now find ourselves is utterly unprecedented. It is not only that various nations, including the presumably civilized and the neo-barbaric, possess the weapons of ultimate destruction—atomic, hydrogen, cobalt, and whatever else may be in process of "perfection." It is more that geography itself, formerly as stable a quantity as one could imagine (the continents and the oceans are still in much the same positions as in the days of Alexander the Great and the Macedonian phalanx), is drastically revised, and so is our national attitude toward the world at large and our own position in it and relationship with it. As Dr. von Neumann has said, "literally and figuratively, we are running out of room." It is difficult to remember that, early in the second world war, important voices were raised—among them the voices of Herbert Hoover and Charles A. Lindbergh—contending that we should build pursuit planes but not bombers for our Air Corps, since pursuit planes might be justified as needed for the defense of our continental boundaries, whereas bombers could be considered only as weapons of offense.

ONLY YESTERDAY—WEAKNESS

These past sixteen years represent the most violent period of change in our entire history as an independent republic. In 1939 we were a relatively weak nation, militarily, determined to isolate ourselves by law from the conflicts of Europe and Asia. In 1939 there were less than 400,000 men in our regular army, navy, and air force combined. Today there are more than 20 million living Americans who have had training and experience in our armed forces, and a large proportion of that experience has been overseas. We were compelled to develop, in an amazingly short space of time, into the most powerful military force on earth—and we have been compelled to continue, however reluctantly, as the unquestioned leader of the free world in the cold war against Communism. Our national interests are desperately engaged along vast perimeters in Europe, Africa, the Middle East, the Far East, and the Arctic. We have had to undergo revolutionary

155

revisions in our thinking about foreign policy, and it is small wonder that we have made mistakes; but we can't afford to make many more.

As this is written, there seem to be some stirrings of hope in the free world, some intimations of "a new dawn." And yet, it is a reflection of this present age of suspense that a writer must be chary of comment on current gestures by the Kremlin in anything that is to be published later than tomorrow morning. Certainly, the leaders of the free world can hardly be blamed if, when they arrive at a Big Four Conference—or a Big Five Conference, including Communist China—they pack in their dispatch cases a healthy supply of skepticism. There is another item of essential equipment that should not be overlooked: maturity. I quote Dr. Vannevar Bush: "Whether we come through the ordeal will depend on whether we are sufficiently mature to map out a wise path and adhere to it. Looking for easy ways, mysterious formulas, or scapegoats will not help."

WE WERE BORN ADULT

I have been told that Pandit Nehru said recently to an American visitor that the U.S. would never formulate a really constructive policy for our relations with Asia until we had achieved the maturity of the British (and Nehru could hardly be classified as an Anglophile). It is almost a basic article in the American credo that Nehru (if he did say that) was right, that ours is a young nation, still afflicted with galloping infantilism, still unable to cope with the old, tempered minds of the Old World. There persists the tradition that cultivated, intellectual American diplomats, such as Dean Acheson or John Foster Dulles, are really ersatz Englishmen in hired striped pants, and therefore easy marks for the genuine article, and that true-blue American statesmen, from the grass roots, are guileless hicks and too innocent to cope with the wiles of foreign city slickers or even to understand their high-falutin jargon.

This idea is abiding but nonsensical. The fact is that there has never been a group of political thinkers, in any one place at any one time, more mature, more urbane, better equipped with long-range vision, than the group to whom we refer proudly as our Founding Fathers. Could one imagine better Ambassadors for any country in any critical period than Benjamin Franklin, Thomas Jefferson, John Adams? Our constitutional system is older, in the consistency of its operation, than that of any of the other great nations of this earth. Our Founding Fathers said, "We hold these truths to be self-evident." But those truths were self-evident to no more than a few advanced thinkers in other countries at that time. In England, in the "Mother of Parliaments," in the period of the American Revolution, the Cabinet was stuffed with the "King's friends" and met as a body only when the King chose to summon it; the then powerful House of Lords was similarly stuffed as well as stuffy; and the House of Commons, dessicated by "rotten boroughs," was ludicrously unrepresentative, bearing scant resemblance to the House that has seen the rise of Winston Churchill. It is not widely understood among Americans today how profound was the effect of our own Revolution on the development of the democratic, constitutional monarchy that has been the strength and the glory of Britain in the past century and a half. And we may find innumerable further evidences all over the world —in such widely divergent states as India and Yugoslavia—of the acceptance of the truths that were held to be "self-evident" for the first time in 1776.

Therefore, it is ridiculous to imagine that we must "grow up" before we can fulfill our imposed mission of world leadership; we were grown up to begin with. Undoubtedly we suffer now and then from adolescent aberrations, and one of the worst of them is the tendency toward xenophobia, the fear and therefore the hatred of anything foreign. This manifests itself in all sorts of ugly, vicious, and even criminal forms, and it also manifests itself in ways that are less blatant but dangerously corrosive to the conduct of our foreign policy. The demand to withdraw from the United Nations and kick that organization out of this country is one of them. This sentiment often approaches the ludicrous, as at a recent Continental Congress of the Daughters of the American Revolution, who sometimes behave officially as if they wished to become the grandmothers of disaster, but it is hardly a laughing matter.

WORLD LAW, WORLD POLICE

In the chapter already quoted, General Sarnoff wrote: "The atom and the electron [in modern war] have made it almost as disastrous for the winner as for the loser. This decisive fact must, in the long run, cancel out war as an instrument of national policy. We cannot know when or what form the coming 'one world' will take, but world law enforced by world police seems inherent in the age of science and technology."

The League of Nations was weak and ineffective for a number of reasons, the chief of which was the refusal by the U.S. to join it. The United Nations is far more effective as a moral force because individual nations are hesitant to incur its censure, particularly since the Korean war; but it has no powers of enforcement. I believe that those powers can be supplied and must be supplied. There seems to be no absolute solution short of "world law enforced by world police." Meetings of the heads of state or the foreign ministers of the great powers can be obviously helpful for the time being to "ease tension," but the essential causes of tension remain and will assert themselves, sooner or later, in one form or another. Tactics of appeasement can be no more profitable than they were at Munich in 1938 and, of course, cultivation of sentiment for "peace at any price" would be an invitation to murder.

Palliatives are not enough to give to the human race the assurance of survival that it requires and, God knows, deserves. The constant threat of a cosmic explosion will remain until there is general disarmament, and there can be no effective disarmament until there are international controls to ensure it.

GREAT RISK, GREAT ACTION

Bold and visionary indeed would be the statesman who would speak out publicly in advocacy of the "one world" concept. He would invite (and receive) screams and imprecations from some members of the Congress, from some portions of the press, from various powerful and influential organizations. But—isn't boldness and vision what we have a right to demand from our leaders? Was there anything less than boldness and vision displayed in the Declaration of Independence, the Constitution, the Emancipation Proclamation? The greatest of our statesmen are those who have not been frightened and rendered impotent by the prejudices of noisy, articulate groups—or by the fear of losing the next election. The greatest of our statesmen have had the courage of their convictions in serving the interests and aspirations of the whole people. Will anybody deny that these interests and aspirations are in and for the attainment of enduring world peace?

The little politician is by nature timorous, ever conscious

of the injunction "Don't stick your neck out!" But the big statesman, regardless of party politics, dares greatly in striving for the highest purpose of the people, regardless of the next election.

"Damn the torpedoes! Go ahead!" are words that express the essential American pioneering spirit. There was a decision, made personally and alone by General Eisenhower, to land in Normandy, on June 6, 1944. The meteorologic staff reported that "the prospect was not bright" for favorable weather conditions but "the consequences of the delay justified *great risk* and I quickly announced the decision to *go ahead* with the attack." (The quotations are from *Crusade in Europe,* by Dwight D. Eisenhower; the italics are mine.)

There is no victory that we could win in the cold war against Communism that would be more decisive than the announcement that our highest authorities are actively and constructively thinking, working, planning for the world that must lie beyond this "plateau of suspense." We cannot promise pie in the sky, but we can give convincing assurance that the moral and physical and intellectual forces of this nation are dedicated to the attainment of our highest aspiration: to find the way to live at peace (as opposed to an "uneasy truce") with our neighbors.

At the fiftieth reunion of the Harvard Class of 1861 Mr. Justice Holmes said: "I learned in the regiment and in the class the conclusion, at least, of what I think the best service that we can do for our country and for ourselves: To see so far as one may, and to feel the great forces that are behind every detail—for that makes all the difference between philosophy and gossip, between great action and small."

"Great action"—that is what our country requires if we are to provide the leadership which may save the world from self-destruction, if anything can.

"There Is No Alternative to Peace"

We run the risk, inevitably, that some peace-seeking action taken by our leaders, even some word spoken, will provoke our enemies to desperation and impel them to strike. We are confronted by ruthless men who have seized enormous power by connivance, conspiracy, assassination—men who live in the atmosphere of terror that they helped to create—men who know that they might lose their power over the minds and bodies of other men if we took from them the initiative in the struggle for world brotherhood and peace.

But what risks are greater than those that we are running already? Damning the torpedoes may have seemed foolhardy at the moment, but it was the only way for Farragut to get into Mobile Bay.

CHARLES P. TAFT

Charles Phelps Taft, son of the former President and younger brother of the late Senator, has been, among other things, a lawyer, lecturer, labor-relations consultant, housing expert, and corporation director. He was the first layman ever elected president of the Federal Council of Churches in America, later helped establish the World Council of Churches. In politics Charles Taft has ranged himself on the "liberal" side of the Republican party, and on the anti-organization side of several memorable fights in Cincinnati and Ohio. He is forever taking on an awesome number of civic chores, one of the most significant in his current portfolio being the presidency of the Committee for a National Trade Policy.

162

The Familiar Men of 1980

BY CHARLES P. TAFT

Can we predict what the world will be like in 1980? We can, of course, make charts of events in the past twenty-five years and from them project trends for the twenty-five years to 1980. This is "extrapolation." But life for the living is not all logarithmic. Some things in life do not change and some change only slowly and unpredictably. We must take account of these, too, in projecting the future.

Does human nature, for example, change? Do we alter our human characteristics observably in twenty-five years? I doubt it. In the next quarter-century, science will undoubtedly advance. Perhaps, as General Sarnoff suggested, we are "on the threshold of the technological age." But even technological progress does not necessarily proceed at a constant rate; I remember in the 1930's complaints that invention, as reflected in U.S. Patent Office records, had slowed down. Productivity, too, will probably continue to improve, but again there is no assurance that the recent high rate of improvement will be maintained. I happen to think it *will* be maintained for the next twenty-five years. Human characteristics, however, have no well-defined trend of improvement, as we were forcibly reminded when the dark abyss of human cruelty opened again under the Nazi and Communist tyrannies.

So we must bring a solid common sense and a healthy skepticism to our projections for the future. Certainly the inertia and the drive of the human spirit must both be taken into account; the triumph of either in the press of events may be pure chance. There was nothing inevitable about the victory of Churchill's spirit in 1940, or the failure of Kerensky's in 1917. Churchill won at Dunkirk, but he lost at Gallipoli in 1915.

Oliver Cromwell said once that one never rises so high as when he does not know where he is going. Cromwell must have been echoing Abraham, who went out not knowing whither he went. But each had his way of looking ahead from the foundations of his past and present, and their lives laid foundations for the future. We must look in the dark glass and try to see through.

DANGLING DESTRUCTION

Will there be war? In today's terms war could mean anything, even to complete and dangling destruction by a cobalt bomb. But I do not think we shall have another global war by 1980. For a number of years I have made this prediction about war with the Russians. Stretching those guesses to twenty-five years is tougher, but I stand by them.

The Russians in their long past have seldom begun a war, although they have nearly always managed to stumble into wars already begun. Their experience on the occasion when they attacked tiny Finland is not likely to encourage another such outburst. The present Soviet leaders, and those most likely to succeed them, are more flexible than Stalin, but they are still doctrinaire and convinced of their ultimate victory. They are unbelievably patient, always probing at supposed weakness, ready to withdraw and bide their time if met by strength.

They are not efficient but they are more efficient than they look. The Germans were beaten in World War II partly because they were deceived by Russia's apparent weakness. For the Russians are great cannibalizers; they steal from one project and ruthlessly divert all their energies to programs that are strategically important, even though in doing so they wreck the cannibalized projects. We must not discount Russian industrial capacity too much.

On the other hand, even the Politburo is not completely free of democratic pressure. Although the Soviet dictators have little regard for human life, even they must take some account of deep Russian characteristics; Stalin revived the Russian Church during World War II. The great danger is that Western policy and intentions may be misinterpreted by party-line informants and that the Soviet leaders may underestimate the will to resist in the free world. Our own actions and intentions must be so clear and unmistakable as to eliminate the chance of any incorrect inferences being drawn in the Kremlin.

The Chinese are less fathomable. They are more isolated than the Russians from the truth of the outside world. Their leaders are even less concerned with human life, and less responsive to any democratic pressures from below. One may doubt if they are as patiently convinced believers in Marxian prophecy.

The countries along China's southern borders, moreover, are far weaker than those on the Soviet periphery. In Southeast Asia subversion and infiltration are the obvious weapons, especially since so many Chinese live in the endangered nations. China has no such capacity as Russia to strike outside her borders with atomic weapons, but she doesn't need it, and she is less vulnerable to atomic retaliation. All these elements add up to greater danger of war.

On the other hand, Chinese logistics, while improving, are bad. Supplies from Russia are still essential for any military operation and the lines of communication are weak. And Russian logistics at home are probably not adequate for any protracted war.

We may not be able to prevent localized wars in the coming quarter-century—even "hot" wars in which our military forces will have to participate. Southeast Asia is the most dangerous spot, again because of the Chinese. The difficult problem there, as in every area, is to build character, honesty, and responsibility as well as the ordinary know-how of political method in the leaders of small new nations. These qualities are earned, not given; we tend to forget how recently—only seventy years ago—corruption was widespread in our own public life in Washington.

I have high hopes that India may yet become a balance to Chinese expansionism. If China's infiltration of India's border provinces becomes too obvious, India, for all her neutrality, will take a firm stand. This is a dark glass, and the view beyond is dark. Perhaps it is only natural optimism that leads me to say, no war with China either.

UP FROM THE BOTTOM

What about the capacity of our own government for dealing with foreign affairs? In recent years the public attitude toward our State Department has reached a low point. I hope we have passed that point and started up, because the effect of such a situation on the morale of our diplomatic personnel is devastating. This has certainly been shown in the severe falling off in applications for entry into the Foreign Service in the last couple of years. I believe the public repute of the State Department will improve during the next twenty-five years, not only because it cannot sink much lower, but because most of the attacks against the department have been unfair and unwarranted. The Foreign Service is, on the whole, a highly competent, professional service of the finest loyalty. To be sure, it needs a certain infusion of outsiders at various levels; a limited number of political appointments is not a bad thing. State should also devise a way to give its men in the Foreign Service six months' contact with American business and community life every few years. And I don't mean in the universities.

The conduct of our foreign relations should continue to improve. The danger of overly military thinking in the executive branch is probably past. A sound man of military background has done better in reorganizing the mechanism of strategy, through a civilianized National Security Council, than did a civilian artillery captain, impressed by military rank. Technical assistance to underdeveloped countries is being improved and reorganized and should become increasingly effective. All the parties involved will learn better in the next twenty-five years how the process actually works, how slowly as well as how fast. We are learning, for example, just how far our own ideas and methods of free enterprise can be applied to countries with a different culture and background, e.g., a private American attempt to get the French to buy their clothes by the semi-made-to-order system was notably unsuccessful.

THE AXLE THAT SQUEAKS

What about domestic policy in the years ahead? Can middle-of-the-roaders continue to control the Congress and the executive branch across party lines, when the two great political parties are so deeply rooted in local jobs and county courthouses and city halls? The personality of Dwight Eisenhower has helped strike the present balance, but his philosophy is apparently shared by a substantial majority of the American people. Can the kind of middle-of-the-road government he represents be kept in power for as long as twenty-five years without his kind of personality in the White House?

One of the great difficulties will be the pressure exerted

by regional groups. The South comprises one and the farm bloc another. I am not foolish enough to suggest that either of these is a completely cohesive group, but each has unity in a broad sense. Each has changed and become complicated beyond belief in the past twenty-five years and there is reason to think the changes will continue. If the changes make for less isolationism and less self-consciousness, and greater homogeneity between regions and between rural and urban groups, that is good.

There is resistance to change in both areas, but the pressure for common thinking is great, too. Mechanization in agriculture, as in business, came about largely in response to the shortage and rising cost of manpower. The shouts of the segregationists in the South today are simply frustrated outcries against the inexorable trend toward more effective use of available skills in the face of competition.

Competition may be one of our idols, but those subjected to it seldom like it. Competition between regions or against foreign producers always evokes cries of anguish, hardly consistent with our business worship of free enterprise. The representatives of a democracy tend naturally to listen to the axle that squeaks. I am afraid that 1980 will be no different. Organizations to represent the broad consumer interest will be just as much needed in Washington in 1980 as today. One may hope, however, that in such fields as trade and tariff policy the extraordinary progress of the past twenty-five years will at least be continued and that the broad general interest will prevail over the cries of the protectionists.

THE POLITICAL JOB

The difficulty in creating a strong middle-of-the-road party lies, as I have said, in the local base of our national political organizations. There is little state organization anywhere.

Tom Dewey was supposed to have the tightest state organization known, but it could not deliver for a good man when Dewey quit. No, the political parties in the states are made up of local satrapies, some effective, some not, some with patriotic and civic leadership, some without.

Will this change? I don't think so. Issues at the state capitals are important, but they are not so compelling as those at either the local or the national level. Consequently it is hard to build up any kind of voluntary political group at the state level, and pressure groups exert their greatest influence there. With few strong state political organizations to contend with, the pressure groups have a heyday in the state capitals. I see no tendency for this situation to change by 1980.

Perhaps at the local level of politics, businessmen and labor leaders will become more active and put in more time. They can more readily do so there because local politics interfere less with the daily chores of business. It is not enough, however, for businessmen to run the money end of political campaigns and appear as members of "advisory committees." Too often the power implicit in the control of party funds is not exercised. Businessmen are content to let the professionals do the work and make the decisions. I wish I thought 1980 would see a big change here.

One trouble, perhaps incurable, is that most business people are unaccustomed to exercising the patience needed to persuade the variety of characters (in all senses) whose votes are needed to support a complicated program. Will businessmen ever really understand, with more democratic feeling than the phrase seems to imply, what J. C. Oliver called the "Endless Adventure of Governing Men"? Perhaps. I see some progress, particularly among the younger generation of businessmen. But on the whole, the trend is discouraging.

The trend in labor-management relations is not much

more encouraging. Some labor leaders today seem intent on reviving the bogeys of the technocrats, who years ago warned us what the shifts to machines, like the cotton picker, would do to employment. These shifts have in fact proved to be valuable readjustments, normal to our dynamic economy. Our extraordinary growth in productivity has made for more jobs, not less; more security, not less; more stability, not less. If we tried by the manufacturing processes of 1794 to make all the textiles that the world uses (and it does not have enough) we would need some 13 billion workers.

THE RETRAINING JOB

We should, of course, do much more in the years ahead to improve worker adaptability. Our public and vocational schools are now generally agreed that they should teach a group of related skills—not just bricklaying or the Morse code—to vocational students. They also recognize the contribution to adaptability implicit in a substantial dose of general education. In the next quarter-century we should see further progress in this direction at the school level.

I am less optimistic that there will be much improvement in the placement and retraining of the workers who are forced to change their occupations. We did not do very well at this during the depression. Of course, jobs were painfully scarce then, but there tended to grow up an ever larger core of "unemployables" who were never reabsorbed until World War II. This job of retraining and placement must probably be undertaken by some agency of government. Businessmen, however, tend to suspect government employment and training agencies and to assume, perhaps justifiably, that such agencies are under the thumb of the labor unions. Thus the kind of community cooperation needed to increase the skills of workers at the second echelon of manpower (below supervisors) is lacking. And since the demand for "unskilled" labor is diminishing, the risk is growing that those out of work may become "floaters" if they are not retrained in new skills.

The absence of adequate retraining facilities has bearing on a bigger problem. Is "full employment" possible during the next quarter-century? This is your bread-and-butter question.

THE FRICTIONAL FRACTION

Obviously it is quite impossible for all persons who want to work to be immediately and simultaneously employed. A certain number of people are always sick, shifting jobs, shifting residences, ceasing to work, beginning to work. This is frictional unemployment. What percentage of the total work force should it represent? Is the present ratio—a little under 5 per cent—too high?

Experience indicates that when unemployment falls much below 5 per cent, and beyond doubt when it falls below 2½ per cent, the availability of many skills in many areas approaches zero. This obviously hurts the economy. It sets up an inflationary force greater than can be compensated by increasing productivity, and the higher prices that result come out of the pockets of those who are working.

A modest amount of frictional unemployment is the price of labor mobility. It was clearly good for New England that in fifteen years it lost 70,000 jobs in textiles while it gained over 400,000 in machine shops, electronics, aviation, etc. United Aircraft, when it was expanding, decided to stay in Connecticut to tap the pool of broadly skilled labor there. And a business bought recently in Ohio was moved back to its purchaser's plant in New England. This is typical of America, and I believe it will continue to be.

Actually, if we can keep unemployment from 1955 to 1980

at 4 to 5 per cent of the labor force, it will be an extraordinary accomplishment, especially after 1960 when the bumper crops of babies born during the last twelve years begin to flood the labor market.

MR. REUTHER'S DILEMMA

What will be the role of organized labor in the next twenty-five years? I happen to believe that if management's personnel practices had improved earlier, unions might never have got their start. Elton Mayo, as director of research at the Harvard Business School, pioneered in sound human relations in industrial organization thirty years ago. But this new knowledge spread slowly, and unions developed largely in reaction to paternalism and inadequate personnel practices.

Now, of course, unions are here to stay. Businessmen have accepted them and are reconciled to negotiating with them. This ought to mean increasingly peaceful and constructive labor relations. I am not sure that it does. The National Planning Association has published studies of a dozen or more companies with long records of peaceful labor relations. In nearly all these companies, however, labor and management met at the plant level; today the trend is increasingly toward company-wide, and even industry-wide, bargaining.

This trend will reduce the democratic participation of local union committees and of local managers and foremen in labor relations. It will intensify the political quality of the national union, increasing the leaders' drive for prestige within the union and as between unions. In the United Auto Workers, for example, if Reuther is not out in front shouting at least as loud as any of his rivals, he may find himself voted out of office. Labor "statesmanship" under such conditions is a bit difficult, to say the least.

THE UNKNOWN ECONOMY

There is too little understanding among politicians and labor people of the resilience of our economy, and of the long-term effectiveness of federal fiscal policy—taxation, budgetary policy, credit regulation, and other indirect controls. These do not work fast enough for the impatient "outs" and the even more impatient politico-labor leaders. The recent inventory depression ran its course and, with sound government help, ended. But this was not achieved without early shouts for the government to "do something" drastic.

Businessmen, for their part, are dismally inarticulate and ineffective in explaining or promoting the free-enterprise system. They are too accustomed to employing "mouthpieces" in their promotional activities. We need more business leaders who will do their own homework. In the entire U.S., the businessmen who can talk effectively to a hostile audience, or persuade an open-minded group not made up of their own associates, can be counted on the fingers of two hands. Most businessmen talk to, and cheer, one another, without really testing their analysis anywhere that it is under attack. They suffer from the occupational disease of inability to listen. It used to be said of Senator Arthur Capper that he could keep both ears to the ground at the same time. That is a necessary quality for a successful political leader, and is equally necessary for a businessman who wants to promote the understanding of sound economics.

Neither do businessmen do a very good job of philosophical analysis of their economic system. One hardly expects from a businessman a performance like Adolf Berle's prob-

173

ing of the modern corporation complex, but only a few busi-nessmen like Beardsley Ruml and Chester Barnard have produced much original thought or persuasive intellectual argument for the enterprise system. And these scattered vol-leys are no match for the constant drumfire of specious eco-nomic argument issued by the labor press.

The real threat of creeping socialism does not derive from government-sponsored welfare programs. Reactionaries still blast such programs—including public housing—but they are now generally accepted by middle-of-the-roaders. The real threat of creeping socialism comes from the general ignor-ance of economics and the exploitation of this by certain labor leaders, politicians, and others. Their arguments run something like this: (1) Monopoly is increasing. (2) Antitrust is good but doesn't stop it; we must have government take over sizable chunks of monopolized industry. (3) This taking over requires planning; business does planning, and so can gov-ernment; government should decentralize its planning, as it did with TVA, and apply the TVA principle to iron and steel and automobiles.

To this is added the purchasing-power theory that seeks to put public money in the hands of consumers but refuses to support measures that would encourage creation of more jobs in private industry. Class war is not promoted per se, but the ill-tempered inheritance from Karl Marx shows up in con-stant attacks on the motives of business leaders.

A FREE AND SASSY PEOPLE

Does all this mean that the socialists, and those labor lead-ers who parrot their arguments, will win out during the next twenty-five years? I don't think so.

In Britain, under the Labor government, there were not

174

enough competent civil servants to do the jobs that had to be done. And Britain's was only a very partial socialism; the nationalization of steel, in fact, was the only radical step taken. In our kind of democracy, the government would be even less likely to attract and hold the kind of men needed to do the planning. For one thing, men of capacity and character would not be likely to obtain the political appointments. As a British economist, who visited this country last year, wrote: "State action that might be fruitful in Britain might be dangerous in America, because of the existence of the spoils system and lobbying."

But in addition to this practical consideration, and no matter how competent public servants might be, centralized judgment in Washington cannot plan for the diversified demands of 164 million people. The burden is too great. Bureaucrats can buy for the government in wartime, and also ration goods during shortages, but they cannot satisfy the free choices of a free and sassy people in peacetime.

One important group of U.S. liberals—our religious leaders —has begun to appreciate this fact. The National Council of Churches in a recent policy paper declared:

"Uncritical recourse to the state to remedy every evil creates its own evil. It may easily become a threat to freedom as well as to efficiency. The union of political and economic power is a dangerous road, whether it leads toward complete state control of economic life, or toward control of the state by private centers of economic power. A wide distribution of centers of power and decision is important to the preservation of democratic freedom."

Thus, a better understanding of economic truths seems to be getting into the minds of more people, and perhaps by 1980 we will see further progress. If the progress is as great as in the last twenty-five years, we will be lucky.

THE CORPORATION'S SOUL

Businessmen have acquired a considerable amount of social consciousness during the past twenty-five years. I am not talking about the so-called public relations or educational activities of individual companies or national trade associations. These are not an effective answer to the labor-socialist attacks. Howard Bowen, writing in the Federal Council of Churches book series on *Social Responsibilities of the Businessman,* describes social consciousness as the expressed obligation of management not only to pay a fair wage but also to help create a sense of vocation and to enhance the worker's personal satisfaction in his job as a human experience. As Bowen points out, the social consciousness of great corporations is promoted by the glare of publicity in which they must operate, and by a management attitude now approaching that of trusteeship, not only for the stockholders, but for employees, customers, and the general public.

But do directors and executives feel they may weigh moral considerations in taking decisions as trustees? Should they, for example, countenance blacklisting of individual workers? And if that practice continues, should industry set up a review board, as Adolf Berle suggests, to hear an appeal when a man is turned down because he is on a blacklist furnished by other employers? A similar situation exists when an employee refuses to answer a government investigating committee on the ground of the Fifth Amendment and this refusal is taken as a cause for discharge without further investigation or hearing. In this field I believe we are going to see a steady enlargement of the corporation's solicitude for employee rights, part of a continuing advance in the ethics and social consciousness of business.

LEARNING TO LIVE

And what about leisure? We must learn to relax more in the coming quarter-century. Most of us have not been taught enough about how to keep fit. Despite the wonders of medical science and the lengthening of the *average* life span, the pressure of modern life is actually shortening the lives of many people. Certainly the men in public life feel an increasing pressure; witness the rising volume of their official correspondence and papers. Teddy Roosevelt's papers number about 500,000. My father's total one million pieces. Franklin Roosevelt amassed one million documents from March 4, 1933, to September 4, 1934, alone.

Another cause for concern is our current preoccupation with the goal of "security." It is exerting a subtle and softening influence on our culture. I am for cultivating security, but I can't agree with the usual definition. For children the important security is love and care. For adults it is not necessarily pay or fringe benefits or even guaranteed employment. It is the certainty of continuing and satisfying human relations with the working group, the social group, the family group. It is something social and spiritual, not economic. I don't mean at all that pay is not important, but Industrial Conference Board studies have shown that employers tend greatly to exaggerate the importance of wages.

I am not sure the present over-emphasis on security will decrease by 1980. Our culture tends to underrate the *spiritual* value of calculated risk-taking. The readiness to meet change, to launch out in an unknown sea—this is not bred in us any more. Perhaps it was always a scarce quality. *"Punch* is not as funny as it used to be," complained a reader to Du Maurier. "It never was," he replied.

Above all, American life needs the ideals of personal in-

tegrity and responsibility characteristic of our American religious tradition. Risk-taking, competition, ingenuity, even
hard work and free choice—the essential constituents of the
enterprise system—all need the moral scrutiny and restraint
that comes from the Puritan conscience.

RELIGION AT WORK

No one could claim that religion has established any dominant influence in our everyday life. But it is certainly true
that religion has grown steadily in influence. At the time of
the first national census in 1790, it has been estimated, only
one American in ten was a church member; the latest census
showed 59 per cent of our people to be church members and
a recent Gallup poll placed the figure at 79 per cent of all
adults.

What is the prospect for religion in the next twenty-five
years? Church membership will probably continue to grow
but, what is more important, the influence of religion should
grow impressively. There is one recent development in
church thought that may assume widespread significance by
1980. The major contribution of the Second Assembly of the
World Council of Churches in 1954 was its emphasis on the
layman and his problems in workaday life. The churches have
too long neglected this area; the worries that kept a man
awake nights in connection with his job were thought to be
none of the Lord's concern. Now the churches are beginning
to promote religious discussion among laymen, and to provide intelligent advice on how the walls of the church can be
stretched to the very limits of the community.

In the education of our children the churches may come to
play an increasingly important role. At present there is no
integrating factor to bind together the bits and pieces of their
learning and give them meaning. The best program of church

education I know is that of Dr. Ligon, of Union College, Schenectady, in which parent and child work together from Monday to Saturday. Although few denominations have picked up the Ligon plan as yet, many individual church schools are trying his methods, with surprisingly enthusiastic parent participation and excellent results.

Will this spiritual renascence change the world by 1980? I think not. We are stuck hard and fast in some dilemmas that offer no satisfactory solution. They will continue to plague us. But it is not unjustified extrapolation to say that it should be easier for laymen to get spiritual help for their tough everyday decisions in 1980. And with such guidance their relations with their fellow human beings should grow more satisfying. This may be a modest goal, but it is a worthy one.

HENRY R. LUCE

Henry R. Luce is the Editor-in-Chief of *Time, Life, Fortune,*
and *Sports Illustrated.* As the technical marvels of the next quarter-century unfold, how will men look on the meaning and the
purpose of earth's greatest marvel, human life? It is left to Mr.
Luce to deal with the most speculative topic of all. Here he
ventures an inquiry into the measureless future of a measureless
force: the human spirit.

180

A Speculation About A.D. 1980

BY HENRY R. LUCE

One day, a year or so ago, Miss Margaret Bourke-White, who in the last decade has been roaming the ends of the earth for *Life,* asked to see me. That meant that she had some big and probably wild and expensive project to propose. I wondered what it could be, for it seemed to me she had already done everything including the North Pole, to say nothing of the darkest depths of coal mines and of Africa. When she came into my office she proceeded in a matter-of-fact manner to register her request. She wanted a promise that it would be she and no other who would have the assignment to go to the moon. Taking her quite seriously, I said yes.

Naturally, we will be happy to have the Trip to the Moon in *Life*—and an analysis of its economic consequences in FORTUNE. But I began to ask myself in the following days: Do I myself want to go to the moon? I mean even after Miss Bourke-White has got back quite safely, and regular service has been established and Pan Am is kicking up an awful fuss because the route has been allotted to an upstart? I have concluded that I do not really care about personally going to the moon. This conclusion has been a little disturbing to me, since up to now there has never been any place that I didn't want to go to. I have never had my fill of traveling this earth and visiting its inhabitants. Human destiny is here—is it not? —and it is this which has fired my curiosity and aroused my

181

concern. But if men and women are soon to be tripping to the moon, that surely will radically change the whole outlook on the human adventure, which will have passed beyond any grasp I might have of its meaning and purpose.

But still, I further reflected, it will continue to be the *human* adventure. And if that adventure does, as I believe, have meaning and purpose; if it is true, as Lord Tennyson sang, that "thro' the ages one increasing purpose runs," then none of us will be alien in any new and vaster age. Occupationally obsolescent I may be; but not personally alien. So—on to the moon! In mental reach, if not in physical fact!

Furthermore, if Lord Tennyson is right, then going to the moon is significant (and it doesn't matter too much if it really is *not* so pretty as Hawaii or so splendid as the Alps). First of all it is significant because man gets there by his own efforts, by the use of his God-given faculties. Second, it is significant because when man gets to the moon, it is because God may want him to get there to see what he has never seen before, to see everything in literally a new light.

THE LIGHT THAT HURTS

How painful it is to see things in a new light! When only a few centuries ago the suspicion dawned with Copernicus that our earth was not the center and greater part of the universe, it was frightfully upsetting. Human life has never been the same since. And when, in our great-grandfathers' time, the Darwinian rumor ran, all too plausibly, that Adam and Eve were not created in B.C. 4532, and that we came from a long line of monkeys—that half-truth brought spiritual derangement to millions. Will God never let us alone for an aeon or two to get used to enjoying the half-lights of the world we have? Evidently not.

The actual day-to-day conditions of human life on this

planet are changing faster in our lifetime than in all times past. And the lights change, the way people see things. Not only the atom is probed, but also the psyche; both are "disintegrated."

With all these shocks of change, the wonder is that we— speaking especially of Americans—hold so firmly to the sense of purpose in human life. Why do we so stubbornly refuse to believe that life is meaningless? Science discloses no "meaning" or "purpose." Our artists and our novelists have disintegrated the human personality into the most miserable shreds of degradation. But we persist in talking of "human dignity." Is our talk a last collective shout in a cosmic graveyard? Twenty-five years from now, will men believe still, or more than ever, that there is in life a "dignity" infinitely precious —that liberty wagered against death will win and is forever worth winning—because indeed "thro' the ages one increasing purpose runs"?

Such questions will never be answered with universal satisfaction. But these are the questions around the answers to which human life has always been organized. The long-gowned Scholar of China, the Christian Knight of Chivalry, the Brahman of India, the Russian Commissar, the Responsible Citizen of America—all of these have been living symbols of the types of organization which have embodied the meaning of life in every civilization.

It is the premise of this article that as the world rushes into ever vaster and more complex organization, the ultimate questions of human destiny, far from being left behind like children's questions about the stork, are likely to become more than ever the primary stuff of human conversation and controversy.

To the ultimate question of whether there is actually any purpose in human life—or any "meaning" beyond the pleasure-pain calculus—there are only two respectable or noble answers, one of which must be false. One answer is: yes, there is a purpose in human life and it is God-given. The other answer is: no, there really isn't except as man invents his own purpose and upholds it.

LORD TENNYSON VS. LORD RUSSELL

The first answer is the Christian or Tennysonian answer generally accepted by Americans today. Our acceptance of the Christian answer is apt to be careless, shallow, and ignorant, both in theory and in practice; but it is the one we are used to; it is the one which, despite our quarrels and uproars, has given to American life and politics a remarkable *consensus*.

The second answer is less familiar to us; it is chilling and even frightening. Americans rarely face up to it; it is contrary to the American ethos. In Europe, the skeptical or atheist position is much more at home. Noble expression has been given to it by the lively eighty-three-year-old mathematician-philosopher, Lord (Bertrand) Russell. Here is one of his many eloquent passages:

"Brief and powerless is Man's life; on him and all of his race the slow doom falls pitiless and dark. Blind to good and evil, reckless of destruction, omnipotent Matter rolls on its relentless way; for Man, condemned today to lose his dearest, tomorrow himself to pass through the gate of darkness, it remains only to cherish, ere yet the blow falls, the lofty thoughts that ennoble his little day; disdaining the coward terrors of the slave of Fate, to worship at the shrine that his own hands have built; undismayed by the empire of chance, to preserve a mind free from the wanton tyranny that rules his outward life; proudly defiant of the irresistible forces that tolerate, for a moment, his knowledge and his condemnation, to sustain alone, a weary but unyielding Atlas, the world that his own

184

ideals have fashioned despite the trampling march of unconscious power."

Lord Russell's stoic view has never sustained any process of civilization. However, if ever there could be a time when the Atlas-Prometheus faith could provide the *consensus* for a civilization, it is the age on which the sun of knowledge and power is now rising so high. By 1980, the whole outlook on life will have so radically changed that there might emerge, for the first time on this planet, an elite capable of sustaining a magnificent civilization (probably global) on the basis of the noble Lord's noble and Promethean philosophy.

THE BREAD-AND-SWEAT EQUATION

Whatever may be the purpose of human life, if any, one thing is clear: that in all past experience human purpose has had to be worked out primarily within the limits of an unbreakable economic equation. That equation was stated in the third chapter of Genesis in terms of a divine command: "In the sweat of thy face shalt thou eat bread." And this command (which was also perfect economic analysis and perfect economic prophecy for all of Toynbee's twenty-one civilizations) was confirmed by the single economic passage in the Lord's Prayer: "Give us this day our daily bread."

In mid-twentieth-century America, bread is a drug on the market. Our problem is not to get bread, but to get rid of it. The breaking of this age-old economic equation is, in the sweep of history, just as new as the atom—and much less appreciated.

From the day when Abraham came out of Ur of the Chaldees, from that day until yesterday, the rule of life has been that one man with the help of his wife and little children, by heavy toil from sunup till sundown, could just barely keep body and soul together. The tiny surplus from his labor went to the overlords and intellectuals for their service in maintaining order and in providing spiritual food; even at the subsistence-survival level, man does not live by bread alone.

In our time this "sweat-of-brow" equation has been radically altered. It was apparent more than one hundred years ago that it would be. The founding of FORTUNE was prophecy, in journalistic terms, that the breakthrough was very near. The Great Depression did not cause us to regret the prophecy. By 1937 we were saying that it was a disgrace that our national income was then barely $75 billion because it could be, right then, $150 billion. That was half again what it had been in the 1929 boom—far more, in other words, than any great number of men had ever known.

It took the war to get America out of its ten-year trance of hypochondria. With the war we took up our bed of impotence and walked and ran and sailed and flew all over the world—as no breed of men had ever done before. And after the war Americans settled down, with much worry and turbulence of talk, to make the FORTUNE figure of a decade before look like gross underestimation of American capacity. FORTUNE's phrase for this phenomenon, before it happened, was "the calculability of abundance." The "calculability" was that Americans could produce all that every American needed for physical well-being—with lots of leisure, amusement, culture, education, etc., thrown in. FORTUNE figured this could be done without any fantastic schemes such as Technocracy; indeed, the surest way to make abundance impossible was to mortgage ourselves to a "planned economy."

QUAINT KILOWATTS

Today we can glimpse the end of the *habit* of poverty— that habit of thinking poorly. And how ridiculous is now that notion, which so recently delighted so many "planners," that

186

mankind would run out of raw materials, including food! Abundance has become visibly the norm of life in America. Having been achieved in America as a human reality, this economy of abundance is likely to become the global condition of man's life on earth.

One more point about the shattering of the economic equation of the third chapter of Genesis. The equation was shattered by *pre-atomic means*. It was the dear little old steam engine and the du Pont chemistry of 1925 vintage and the simple electricity of those quaint old utility tycoons—these simple, straight-forward Newtonian tools were enough to change utterly the physical condition of life on earth.

And now comes the atom. In a previous chapter Dr. John von Neumann of the Atomic Energy Commission summarized the whole thing in one stroke: by 1980 all "power" (electric, atomic, solar) is likely to be virtually costless. In von Neumann's vivid phrase, power will be "free like the unmetered air."

Now faced with the superabundance of atomic technology, we Americans have just barely experienced the pre-atomic abundance; most of mankind cannot imagine, does not actually comprehend, what we already possess. And we ourselves are certainly not *used* to it. Our imagination—that is, the way we think of the world and ourselves and others and how we live our lives—lags far behind the objective reality of the circumstance of abundance. And having not yet had time to learn how to live and think in one new economic world, we are already walking into another, newer, stranger, greater.

LOST GYROSCOPE

The age-old subjection of human life to an economic equation has had consequences in the mores of every civilization. Consider just one large example in the cultural history of

the West: the ideas and the mores associated with **Calvinism.**
The Calvinist cosmology put a high spiritual value on productive (economically valuable) work, work being not only
salutary in the sense that idleness leads to sin, but more profoundly in the sense that through work man can exercise his
personal responsibility, can, in St. Paul's phrase, "work out
his own salvation." This ethos—this deep belief in the moral
imperative of work and of personal responsibility—is still a
driving force in America. What will happen to America
when work seems not to be the gyroscope of morality? Old-
sters have been shaking their heads about this for a long
time.

Meanwhile, now, at this moment, we are in a transition
stage between the Calvinist work-imperative and the von
Neumann "free power." And we have pretty well matured
our social ideal for this pre-atomic age of abundance. We call
it "a decent life for all." To us this seems both natural and
realistic; it is a balanced compound of work (production) and
pleasure (consumption). Specifically, our social ideal has this
bill of fare: enough food and clothes and housing for everyone
to live healthfully (with plenty of medical care and wonder
drugs and a life expectancy of one hundred years), and *also,*
for everyone, the means of consuming a full diet of education
and culture. Why not?

Now, I must ask forgiveness if I seem to speak of this "decent life for all"—and culture, too—in a disparaging or trivial
sense. It is a magnificent thing, more splendid perhaps than
all the cathedrals ever built. It is the realization of the hopes
of all the thousands of servants and lovers of mankind who
for the last two hundred years have given their lives to free
mankind from its misery, to make forever untrue Hobbes'
famous definition of human life as being "solitary, poor,
nasty, brutish, and short." Plagues—as a boy I was in a plague

188

where they carried the dead out to be burned on huge pyres every night for months; plagues, famines—I have seen the bloated abdomens of children whose mothers lay dying on the wayside; plagues, famines, mass hysterias, superstitions, fanaticisms, the brutalization of nineteenth-century industrial workers—all these miseries and cruelties, with wars hardly any worse than peace, have been the "fate" of man. To rid mankind of these monstrous offenses, to smash the false ineluctabilities of fate, and to put in the place of all this awfulness a decent life, a life of air and light and chosen food and education and recreation and length of years—this summarizes the efforts and the prayers of some of the truest heroes of mankind for the past hundred and fifty or two hundred years. Let the heroes rejoice that their warfare has been successful, that their goal is in sight. And let us give thanks that we have inherited their victories, far beyond our own deserving.

W H Y ?

But—and there is a but—there is a wonder and doubt whether this ideal of "a decent life for all" is good enough. Why the doubt? Divine discontent does not really explain it —unless one asks why discontent should be inextricable from human nature and why it is recognized as precisely the divine within us. The truth is that *no conceivable utopia on earth will satisfy man.* However profoundly compelling is the urge to overcome whatever misery and brutality there is, and to substitute for it a man-conceived utopia of workless prosperity and global peace—no such utopia will satisfy even in the imagination, much less in the realization.

So, I speculate that a consequence of the economy of abundance which now is—and even more a consequence of superabundance to come—may be that men and women will experience a more direct and inescapable confrontation with the ultimate questions concerning the meaning of human life and its purpose. If prosperity and security will not satisfy, what on earth will? Answer: nothing.

What then *is* the purpose of life? Who invented this impossible puzzle or how did it ever come to be? We may shove the question away while contenting ourselves with three-day weekends and practical discussions about World War III. But by 1980, World War III will have happened or been bypassed: even if that fantastic war happens, what is already in the mind of man will go on; "reconstruction" will take place; by 1980 superabundance and some kind of global order will have been established and one great question will abide: why? Trips to the moon will not abate the naked urgency of this question: they will only confront man all the more with the meaning of his existence in the whole light-year cosmos. The confrontation is predictable; whether men in 1980 will have the grace and intellectuality to cope with it is unpredictable.

FREEDOM FROM GOD

"If God did not exist," said Voltaire, "it would be necessary to invent Him." Then another brilliant Frenchman, Auguste Comte, an idol of his age, proclaimed that God was no longer necessary because in fact man *had* invented Him. Surveying the amazing triumphs of intellect and science even one hundred years ago, when there were hardly any railroads (and no plumbing, but much filth and lice), Comte was in an ecstasy of joy over the final Victory of Man. Man had himself conceived the good, the true, and the beautiful, and now that man had at last fashioned the key to truth, namely Science, it was only a matter of a short while before a universal utopia of the good, the true, and the beautiful would envelop the world. In token whereof Comte generously elected Moses,

Homer, Aristotle, and various other well-known characters to a universal Hall of Fame—but not Jesus, whom he disliked.

In the lifetime of many of us now living, H. G. Wells was a lively and attractive prophet of the same utopia. Alas, Wells died at the age of eighty, confessing most pitiably his utter disillusion and despair. Somehow, he confessed, he had been quite wrong about the nature of things, including human nature. The world, instead of coming under the rule of Wellsian Scientist-Kings, had lapsed into what Churchill designated as history's most terrible and most unnecessary war.

But long before the world wars, Nietzsche, perhaps the profoundest prophet of nineteenth-century Europe, had cried: "God is dead." That seemed to fit the facts. God, it seemed to say, had formerly been among us, guiding man, through many a travail, to a certain humanness of kindness and courtesy and honor. But all that was just a kind of childhood of our prodigious race. Nietzsche foresaw the emergence of Superman. He scorned the littleness and meanness of unheroic aristocracy and of bourgeois aims and proclaimed a holy war, not between sects or classes but a war of liberation. The war was to be waged by man, the glorious reality, against God, a debilitating fiction; Nietzsche was a Promethean, a Russellite with drums and banners.

The wild sayings of prophets are not the language of the people, nor of statesmanship, nor of business. Yet both Comte and Nietzsche and the charming Wells are truly representative men—representative of the tides of circumstance and the gusts of feeling which have swept over Europe in the last one hundred and fifty years.

These half-true imaginings of "boundless better and boundless worse" had a plain cause. That cause was Science. And along with Science there was Democracy or, in Ortega y Gasset's striking thesis, the "revolt of the masses." The masses, he

191

said in 1930, were propagating and swarming and revolting. They were indeed—and still are.

The psychic impact of Science and Democracy was, and is, far greater in Europe than in America. This was partly because America itself was a new thing and we ourselves were a new people. To us, for example, faith in God did not seem incompatible with a new way of life. Quite the contrary: it was characteristic of Americans to think of creating, under Providence, a better life than Europe had ever known. In the beginning America was a project—a series of projects. It still is. From the *Mayflower* or the Virginia Company, to the newest baby born at the end of the Oregon Trail, America and the Americans are a host of projects united in the general project of realizing on earth, as Whitman said, all the moral imperatives of the ages.

The question is whether this faith in the tremendous purposefulness of American life—and hence of life everywhere on this planet—can be sustained for the next twenty-five years.

Today, there is still, as we say, a lot to be done and, in America, plenty of will to do it. First of all, we seem wonderfully united in a determination to keep going, to maintain the tremendous economy we have. Furthermore, the economy of abundance does not yet include everyone. There are slums to tear down and cities to rebuild. Furthermore, even the American who is part of the economy of abundance, and knows it, feels that he could do with a bit more: ask the budget-conscious housewife. As for the rest of the world, the job of creating abundance has hardly begun. So, even without going beyond the realm of economics, there is no lack of "challenges" demanding purposeful "responses."

But remember that Professor Toynbee's famous formula

does not assume that *response* will equal *challenge;* his formula ends in a question mark. And in any case I am not sure his formula is correct. It seems to me that the Toynbeean formula is equally true, in fact truer, if it is put just the other way around: the *creative response comes before the challenge.* In the beginning is The Word; what Toynbee calls *"response"* might be better understood as man's choice of goals and purpose. The choice of goals is limited by circumstance and necessity but the significant fact is that the choice is also a "free will" choice. Thus, for example, the miracle of Greece is not explainable as a mere response to certain difficulties; far more compelling is Professor Jaeger's interpretation: that there arose out of Homeric times the ideal of excellence—*arete.* It was not any uniquely useful obstacle which produced the Greek ideal; it was the ideal of *arete* which coped with the primitive local material and, centuries after Ajax and Achilles, produced Pericles and Praxiteles.

As we Americans stand now, emerging from the age of work-imperative and entering an imaginable age of "free power," the question must be asked whether the sense of purpose which spurred the achievements of the past century or two will also incite the next generation to perform the vast work which has yet to be done.

To be sure, we can always count on a full quota of "selfish" motivations. Indeed, never in history has the desire for material goods and even for sheer survival been so appealed to as in our time. The modern potency of "selfish" motivation (including survival, the most "selfish" of all) seems to make irrelevant any concern with ideal purposes which, in any case, in the modern idiom, are suspected of being "insincere."

But I argue that men are not moved solely or even primarily by materialistic motives of gross self-interest. Certainly, the history of the last hundred or two hundred years

193

in the West cannot be read in materialistic terms. If the economic progress of the nineteenth century rested heavily on the dynamism of individualistic "selfish" interests, it was accompanied all along the line by the greatest display the world has ever seen of the altruistic, of humanitarian ideals in action. It was not simply that Carnegie and Rockefeller ended up as philanthropists; the point is that even as the rugged individualists pursued their rugged ways, thousands of other Victorians and post-Victorians devoted their lives to the "social gospel" and achieved every kind of humanitarian reform from the abolition of slavery to the forty-hour week and hospitals and free education. What we have been seeing in America and partially elsewhere—a phenomenon without historical precedent—is the merging of the gospel of work ("free enterprise") and the social gospel ("humanitarianism"). The merging of these two vast rivers with the third river of Science has made the sea of abundance around which the Western World now lives.

MARX NEEDED CHRIST

Paul-Henri Spaak, the great socialist, said in one of his most eloquent speeches that no political party in Europe could claim a monopoly of the Christian tradition. He wanted to claim a fair share of it for himself and for his anticlerical and even atheistic socialists. And Clement Attlee often observed that British Socialism owed more to Christ than Marx. It is not necessary to claim that Christianity uniquely inspired the ideals of humanity and liberty but one must be stubbornly blind not to see the Sign of the Cross above the victories of the social gospel and of political freedom, which is constitutional "liberty under God." One must be blind indeed not to see Communism as a Christian (not a Buddhist or Hindu) heresy. One must be blind indeed not to see that the godless French Revolution could have happened only within Christendom; and in fact nowhere have "liberty, equality, and fraternity" been proclaimed save where the Gospel light has shone. So, even in the heresies which have so nearly destroyed it, the power of the Christian faith is revealed in history.

However much the progress of liberty and fraternity may owe to those who denied God, it owes far more to the unnumbered tens of thousands, great and humble, who have devoted their lives to human welfare in the simple and literal belief that "inasmuch as ye have done it unto one of the least of these my brethren, ye have done it unto me."

"RESTATING" THE ETERNAL

The most specific question to be asked therefore is whether the Christian faith, which has so much inspired and guided us, will still inspire and guide us in those greater works that must be done. And what answers can there be? The simple Christian answer knows that the faith will endure till the end of time but it does not know how effective it will be in shaping history in any particular period; Christianity may become once again the mustard seed hidden in the catacomb of civilization. This is the simple and ineffable answer. But there is another more complex answer which more narrowly concerns us, namely, that the Christian gospel must be preached in every tongue, that is to say *it must be preached in the different language of every different age.* How may it be preached and apprehended in 1980? Or even now in 1955?

Today throughout the Western World (throughout the whole of modern worldwide Westernizing Civilization) there is spectacularly lacking a Christian faith which is both a personal commitment and also a widely accepted explanation

195

of human life and purpose. Efforts to "restate" the Christian faith have been going on for decades. In the social field, these reformulations, both Catholic and Protestant, have had their victories. In the political field there is some partial success: the Christian Democratic movement tries to recreate in Europe a consensus of Christian humanism; and in America, President Eisenhower and Secretary Dulles assert the moral basis of foreign policy, though the effort to relate politics to the moral law is widely opposed, resisted, and sneered at.

But the crucial area is neither politics nor sociology; the crucial area is in men's sense of total reality. The "restatement" of Christian faith most urgently needed is in terms of the new kind of universe which science has been revealing and which even the "common man" apprehends as reality as he steps on his accelerator or flicks his dial.

THE ROCK AND THE ROCKS

The conflict of science and religion, which so agitated our parents, is no longer a major topic in America. Another Scopes trial is hardly a possibility. Today the Scopeses, and the Bryans and Darrows too, understand that they do not have to make a choice between knowing the age of rocks and the Rock of Ages. We have come to the realization that science and religion are two distinct worlds, in which different "affairs" go on. The two worlds are not in substantial conflict. Border incidents crop up from time to time, but the general atmosphere is one of peace. Perhaps "armistice" would be a better word than "peace." For, while we have got science and religion fairly well distinguished from one another, we have not yet got them cooperating with one another. Where there should be only distinction, there is separation. The two affairs go on unrelatedly, whereas they should go on unitedly. The result is a certain impoverishment of both the religious and the scientific enterprise. The man of faith fails to know the full truth about this terrestrial universe, which is the concern of science. Conversely, the man of science fails to know the full truth about the destiny of man, which is the concern of religion. Yet man himself—whether he be savant or simple—pursues his destiny within the horizons of this terrestrial universe. And if the two knowledges proper to the two worlds of science and religion are completely divorced, man will lack the kind of picture of himself-within-the-universe that can unite his mind, his hope, and his conscience in the service of some intelligible, confident, and lawful purpose, place him at home in a harmonious universe of truth, and assure him that all his terrestrial tasks have their final consecration from the fact that they further a destiny that is not terrestrial.

A FRENCHMAN'S GLIMPSE

Such a picture of man is by no means unimaginable; and there are already notes and sketches for it in our age. One such was glimpsed in 1947 by the great French scientist, Lecomte du Noüy, author of *Human Destiny*. There is in this closely reasoned book an almost maternal urgency to recall the lost children of Christendom to their proper spiritual home. Science, he said, which had undermined religion, must now be invoked to restore religion to its rightful place and man to his rightful dignity. Reason does not "prove" God any more than beauty or goodness does. But Reason testifies to God; and without God, Reason becomes madness.

Du Noüy takes evolution as the framework of his argument. First of all he demonstrates that evolution could not "have just happened." The mathematical chances are billions to one against that. Evolution was a response to the divine

197

will. Man arises from within the evolutionary process, and at a certain moment, say the Cro-Magnon age 30,000 B.C., man became truly man by a *mutation* when God breathed into him a "free will," a capacity and duty to choose between "good" and "evil," that is to say, a conscience. Human dignity, says du Noüy, rests on a new mechanism born with conscience—namely, free will—*which orients evolution in a spiritual direction*. Then, surveying all the vastitudes of time and space, du Noüy is able to see man's place and purpose in precisely *that* universe. He says: "The respect for human personality is based on the recognition of man's dignity as a worker for evolution, as a collaborator with God . . . Not only his own fate but the fate of evolution is in his hands."

Collaborators with God in charge of evolution! This *is* a new vision. But there is something familiar about it, too. Perhaps the familiar and the new are both significant.

On the one hand, "collaboration with God" would almost perfectly define "the American religion"—the religion so easily condemned as overoptimistic, complacent, and shallow. The American word, before evolution, was Providence. While on the one hand the American was open to Infinity (cf. Emerson and Whitman), on the other hand he busied himself with a concrete and limited task. The common task, besides individual salvation, was the winning of a continent and the making of a nation dedicated to a proposition. Now we must see this task as having been a limited one, perhaps even accomplished. And while judging "the American religion" to be parochial, and lacking in the sense of tragedy, may we not also see it as a primitive, crude prefiguring of the du Noüy vision?

Collaboration with God in the whole of evolution—this is a vision so new that it may even be regarded as dangerous in its sweep. For it is nothing less than at last to Christianize

198

A Speculation About A.D. 1980

Atlas, to unchain Prometheus on his own recognizance, to create a greater Renaissance which shall not become pagan, and to suffuse Lord Russell's dark, icy cosmology with the light and warmth of Christian love and sacrifice and hope.

Evolution, to be sure, has long since become an inbred thought pattern of the Western World. But we have not yet seen the generation which feels itself personally responsible for an evolution "spiritually oriented." Will we see that generation in 1980? Is it possible that in 1980, some men, and, in a sense, all men, going about their ordinary business, coping with their trivial troubles, will nevertheless see themselves in such a light? It seems impossible; it seems, that is, that for such a vision to take hold of men, a "new" human nature would be required—a new mutation! Yet there are already straws in the wind; there are the signs of the times which we are commanded to read.

COOPERATIVE MAN

Among the signs of the times which we are required to read are some facts about the present condition of man, even about the present *nature* of man, which are quite as striking as the facts of science. One fact which I select for emphasis is the fact that man in our time and especially in America has become cooperative man. Foreign writers on America, whatever their other insights, all agree on the spirit of cooperativeness that pervades American life. Tocqueville in a famous passage noted this long ago; just the other day, in a French business magazine, another observer exclaimed, "They train them, they educate them to cooperate!" The habit and spirit of voluntary cooperation form the ideal base for Organization. Today, to a degree never before known, man is Organized Man.

The fact of ever "higher" and more complex organization manifests itself everywhere on this planet. The most obvious acceptance of the idea of organization is in the economic field —in the belief of every nation that an economy of abundance can be organized. No longer does "Fate" decree that anyone should starve. Certainly, millions will suffer both of starvation and of worse than starvation because of illusions about organizational magic and because of the exploitation of this vision by politicians and rulers. The point here is that the efficacy (and the moral worth) of organization for the satisfaction of wants is now a universal article of faith—an article of faith held as deeply and instinctively as any myth recorded in the *Golden Bough*.

The outstanding instance of cooperative organization is the U.S. To be sure, organization of some sort is essential to all forms of society. The naturalist reveals to us the wonder of the ants and the bees. The anthropologist entrances us with his reports on a thousand forms of organization from tribal cannibals to poetic Mayans. But the organization of *homo Americanus* makes all previous types of organization, including the Roman Empire, appear simple and naive.

The Roman Empire in its prime organized scarcely 50 million people, scattered from the Caspian to Britain; perhaps a third of them were slaves and all but a fraction were poor, ignorant, and short-lived. The American Organization is not only vastly more complex, abundant, and humane, but also incomparably more free. Americans believe—and nothing has proved us wrong—that Organization with freedom, however untidy, is in every way superior to Organization by tyranny, however benevolent. This choice was made long ago and has been vindicated by our faith and by our experience.

200

A Speculation About A.D. 1980

THE TENTH WONDER

Organization today means that virtually every turned water faucet in the land will yield water; that La Guardia's 600 or 800 planes per day will rise or land about when the timetable says they will. A flood, an accident, a hurricane, briefly disrupting this fantastic interwoven reliability, throws briefly into the newspapers a few names, previously unheard of, around whose jobs the continuity broke or was mended; then all goes on as before.

The American Business Corporation typifies (though it by no means exhausts) the American capacity for High Organization. It was born of the freedom of "rugged individualists" to indulge their private greed, exuberance, or Calvinist morality, and of the freedom to move of the ex-European peasants who with shovel, crowbar, and hope once did the corporation's sweaty work. Their children now do its skilled and semiskilled work and a lot more besides. For its growth the modern business corporation depended on an environment of political freedom, and the larger it grew the more it discovered a new dependence on freedom of other kinds as well. It came to require free, responsible individuals within itself, and within its several million brother corporations, for the decentralization of the millions of daily decisions which High Organization implies. Without these millions of diffused but responsible decisions, High Organization would be an inverted pyramid, top-heavy and impossible to sustain. The vast, continuous, and reliable Organization that permeates our expanding economy becomes more anonymous, more decentralized, more dependent on more free, responsible individuals every day.

Having organized production and distribution as the ninth wonder of the world, the modern corporation now finds a

201

new subject for its organization prowess: itself. It is now organizing itself, quite self-consciously, as a responsible social unit. It is publicly and even noisily concerned about its responsibility to its employees, its customers, its stockholders, the city or cities it dwells in, its "public relations," its share in the support of education, culture, patriotism. It subscribes to the symphony and helps its executives' wives get their kids into college.

The corporation's self-organization as a social unit has gone so far that it may be going too far. In place of the old indictment of business as antisocial, its newer critics (for instance, William H. Whyte Jr. in FORTUNE) express the fear it may have bitten off more social responsibility than it can chew. The "moralization of business," hopefully preached by the social-gospelers of a generation ago, has been achieved at least to this extent: whereas the old "soulless corporation" used to proclaim its own honesty and legality, and let it go at that, today it accepts responsibility for every aspect of the social environment on which it impinges. That is a large order, largely self-imposed.

Is it too large an order for the corporation? If so—if the corporation is checked in its career of unlimited altruism— then other forms of High Organization will snatch the torch. They are already in the field. Visualize, for example, not only vast bureaucracies (state, federal, and local) and labor unions, but also universal education and the *organized concern* for education and for mental health and a thousand other matters, and indeed for "cultural" advancement generally.

But the degree and breadth of High Organization we now see are nothing to what we will see. Even today, Dr. von Neumann tells us, the main problem facing technology is this: it hasn't enough room on earth for its own appropriate organization of products and services. The largest nation, perhaps even the whole world, is too small a staging area for the demonstration of what Science can really do with Nature.

The future of Organization, then, must be at least a world-spanning future, perhaps involving the moon and several planets as well. In other words, the vast, complex, subtle, flexible, and efficient organization of men and means in America today must become still more vast, complex, subtle, flexible, efficient, and interrelated.

This is a horrifying prospect to many sensitive people. "Down with conformity"—this is the idealists' cry today; and it has merit. The worry is not only about civil rights, but about the dangerous leveling of thought and standardization of feeling; about the effects of a mass press, mass entertainment, and mass-advertised ways of living, of which TV is only the most recent example. The same wise and sensitive people who yesterday preached social consciousness to the individual are today trying to rescue individuality from a too-well-organized social conscience. Poets and thinkers who earlier wooed the embrace of the downtrodden masses now flee the tread of the organized crowd.

VIRTUE TURNS HABIT

In any case, we've got it—social consciousness organized on a scale never attempted before. And before we flee or condemn it, let us appreciate what we've got. We have made a turn in the development of human nature. We have brought to birth that cooperative society, or a reasonable facsimile thereof, which Kropotkin foresaw in his answer to Darwin. And quite apart from its many practical advantages, this cooperative society records the habituation of many virtues as well. Consider what a cooperative society—*alias* organization with freedom—demands and implies. Merely to conduct our business with each other, whether corporate, private, or governmental, we take for granted mutual good faith, honesty, candor, responsibility; we expect (and often get) conscientiousness, tolerance, understanding; we reasonably hope for a shared purpose and concern. It would take a monstrous calamity to uproot these habit-virtues; but until or unless that calamity comes, we can surely call these virtues an achieved characteristic of our civilization.

But still there is the question: what about the individual? And first let it be said, there is no reason to assume that abundance, safety, comfort, and wide cultural opportunities will of themselves crush the individual in the society of 1980. There will be conflict between society and the individual, as there always has been, and it will not be resolved. But the anarchy that kept the cavemen from venturing out without a club, or even Dr. Johnson from walking the unlit streets of eighteenth-century London unarmed, is surely not more propitious for the development of the individual than the social order I am forecasting. Secure in his person, his larder, and his opportunities, the individual of 1980 can start his private quest from a higher plateau of earthly human achievement. His quest will lie upward still.

President Whitney Griswold of Yale spoke a few years ago of "man's immemorial effort to find his place as an individual in a world that seems to recognize him only as a species." "Since that moment, lost in the mists of time," said Griswold, "when man first looked upon himself and saw the image of God, he has struggled against all the powers of nature and the supernatural, and against all the tyrannies of his fellow man, to fulfill the promise in that image. He has lived to the full, in pleasure and pain, the gregarious life to which half of his instincts and appetites committed him. And in response to the other half, he has striven in every

204

element on earth, in the skies above the earth and in the waters under the earth, to express himself as an individual."

It was the inspired individual—*his* dreams, *his* indignations, *his* inventions—who created our present society, just as past society (both its "good" and its "bad," its ignorance and its treasured wisdom) helped shape him. And just as all biological mutations must start in some unforeseeable organism, so the mutations in human nature that mark the evolution of man must start with one or a few individuals, who in a manner beyond our understanding become possessed of and by the ideal to be proclaimed, the new vision of the eternal logos. Dante was no mere cock crowing at some "inevitable" dawn of the Renaissance; he was a shaper of the Renaissance; he did help make that sun rise; he was a collaborator with God.

But he was not the only collaborator then or before or after. For then as now and in the future, there is not only the inspired individual, there is also the humble servant of truth, the individual servant of charity. And the gifts of the Spirit are various: there is foresight and imagination; there is also duty and tradition. For if, as we believe, the Spirit is at work in the race of man, then the work of the Spirit is done not only in the atom of the individual but also through the generations of men and in traditions and in treasured wisdom and in the moral law slowly apprehended and in the beloved community and in the Church.

While we indeed require individuals who are, as we say, "ahead of their time," we may also liken the hosts of the Spirit to an army having its advance scouts but also its main body of faithful and even, importantly, its rear guard, guarding against backsliding, guarding what has been won at such cost. With this simile, may we not also say that at any given moment—in 1980, say—all the elements of the army have a common sense of where they are despite the continuous cacophony of argument? In 1980 the sense of spiritual geography may be characterized by a wider consciousness of responsibility for the spiritual evolution of that special creation into whom was breathed ages ago the meaning of these very words: responsibility, spirit.

That creation was taught and learned to pray both together and alone, at the altar and in the chamber. In one of mankind's books of common prayer, this is prescribed for priest and for congregation at morning service and evensong:

Minister: O God, make clean our hearts within us.

Answer: And take not thy Holy Spirit from us.

As long as that prayer continues to go up and continues to be answered, we need never fear the greatest triumphs nor the most amazing victories.